The Holy Injil

In Modern English

The Good News
According to Luke

Holy Injil: The Good News According to Luke. First edition.

ISBN 978-0-9913889-7-4

To purchase individual copies of this book visit Amazon.com.
For bulk purchases contact the publisher at luke.injil@gmail.com.

If you have comments or questions see www.Holy-Injil.net or contact the publisher at luke.injil@gmail.com.

Contents

Preface

The Most Famous Book in the History of the World

The Bible is the most famous book in the history of the world. The most translated, the most printed, the most distributed, the most loved, the most read. It is also the most hated and the most vilified. Either way, to be ignorant of it is to be ignorant of history, of religion, of literature, and ultimately of humanity itself.

English translations of the Bible outnumber those in any other language. Historically, they have been designed for people whose religious conceptions were influenced by Latin, the dominant language of Western Europe in the Middle Ages. This translation is for those whose religious conceptions have been influenced by Arabic, the dominant language of Western Asia and North Africa for well over a millennium.

The English word *Bible* ultimately derives from the name of an ancient city, Byblos, once located on the eastern coast of the Mediterranean. Papyrus reeds were there made into "paper" and exported. In Greece, books written on this paper became known as *biblion*, a form of which eventually gave rise to the English word *Bible*.

The translation provided here is part of the Bible, also known as "the Holy Scriptures," or "the Scriptures." Specifically, this selection is from what is often called the New Testament. The selection was written by Luke, a first-century physician and historical investigator. Luke interviewed those who knew Jesus Christ, or Isa al-Masih as he is known in the Arabic world.

English speakers borrow the term *Christ* from Greek via Latin. The equivalent term in Arabic, *Masih*, is related to the Old Testament Hebrew word *mashiah* and means "anointed one," a title used for kings and priests. Luke wrote in Greek, the lingua franca of his day, and his text was called *euangelion*, meaning "good news." In English it became *evangel*, via Latin *evangelium*. The Old English translation of the term was *gōdspell* ("good" + "news"), which later became *gospel*. In Arabic, the Greek term became *Injil*, where it also serves as the name of the New Testament. For those influenced by Arabic, Luke's work is therefore the Injil (or part of the fuller New Testament Injil) about Isa al-Masih, now the most famous person in human history.

The translation provided here was first done in traditional English. Arabicized forms of certain names and terms, like those above, were then selected for English speakers whose religious vocabulary tends to be Arabic. Central to that is the name or reference for the deity. English "God" is a Germanic word found in languages throughout northwestern Europe. Arabic-influenced speakers of English may use that term, but most are more inclined to say *Allah*, a Semitic term related to Hebrew words for God. Middle-Eastern followers of Isa, some of whom trace their origins back to the first and second century A.D., generally call the God of the Bible *Allah*.

The purpose of this publication is to show respect to Arabic-influenced English speakers. They live around the world, they number in the hundreds of millions, and they deserve a translation of the Holy Scriptures designed for and dedicated to them.

About the Translation Methodology

As literal as possible, as free as necessary.

So goes the motto. It's clever and hard to dismiss, but it's difficult to apply.

Without care, translators who try to be "as literal as possible" often end up creating a nasty tasting stew of obscurity and ambiguity. Publishers may promote such a text, and those who know the source language may praise it. But the so-called "accuracy" of literal translations means nothing when the audience is confused. A committed reader may swallow such a stew. To the intensely committed it might even become a steady diet. But we do better to ask if it's both healthy and palatable. In terms describing literature, is the translation clear, compelling, and relevant?

The motto's "as free as necessary" second half is also hard to apply. Languages continually change, dialects divide, and flavors of speech approach the number of speakers. More insidious, freedom can open the way to a mere itch for something fresh or flashy. Straight speech deserves respect for its clarity and power. So even on the creative side, translators must ask themselves if potential additions—implied information, figures of speech, explanatory content and the like—are truly central to the marriage of message and reader. If not, such devices risk becoming like labels on a designer product. Translators must be particularly careful with religious texts. A holy book is a divine inspiration, not a translator's masterpiece.

"As literal as possible, as free as necessary." Balance is a difficult and maybe impossible goal. But translators try, convinced of the power of old truths in new tongues and modern forms. With all that to consider, and in prayerful and humble reliance upon the Almighty, here is the basic methodology of this new version:

1. Translate directly from the original language texts (Hebrew, Aramaic, and Greek), with reference to versions in other languages, especially English.
2. Translate the meaning of the whole, not simply its parts. A look at any dictionary proves that words in isolation have many definitions. Only meaning—words, phrases, sentences in a specific context—can be translated from one language to another.
3. Divide multi-clause sentences into shorter units.
4. Clarify relations between phrases, clauses, and sentences.
5. Clarify ambiguous syntactical constructions, such as genitive ("of") phrases and locative ("in") phrases.
6. Points 1-5 may be summarized this way: Given that there is no

translation without interpretation, fully carry out and represent the hard work of interpretation.

7. Employ active verbs wherever possible, noting the subjects (agents) and objects (patients).
8. Select clear, modern English vocabulary. Many older terms, though sometimes much loved, are easily misunderstood or no longer in general use.
9. Keep figures of speech intact when they were "alive" to the original audience and still communicate clearly in English. Otherwise, modify the figure so it communicates today.
10. Include explanatory footnotes, with the caveat that they represent only a fraction of the many issues faced in translation.
11. Display a broad variety of English literary styles consistent with the variety of the original text.
12. Points 7-11 may be summarized this way: Create a text that is beautiful, reflecting the vast vocabulary and literary tradition of English, and powerful, releasing the truth for people today.

The goals of this version are as simple as A, B, C:

A) An accurate translation, reflecting the original text as inspired by the divine author.
B) A beautiful translation, reflecting the language of today's audience.
C) A clear translation, reflecting the majesty, might, and mystery of Allah, the most compassionate and most merciful.

Topical Articles

Following the text of the *Good News According to Luke*, this edition contains a series of topical articles explaining more about the message of the Scriptures as a whole, the Injil, and its central figure, Isa al-Masih. This section can be viewed as answers to frequently asked questions (FAQ).

These articles quote the Scriptures extensively. Quotations from *Luke* are taken from the translation of Luke in this book, the Mantalaan Translation [MT], copyright © 2015. Unless otherwise noted, the same is true of all other selections from the Holy Scriptures.

In the smaller number of places where other versions of the Holy Scriptures are cited, they are clearly noted by their abbreviation. They are reproduced directly from published books and electronic sources available to the public. Those translations are:

NET, the New English Translation [2006]
NIV, the New International Version [1984]
NLT, the New Living Translation [2011].

Blessing

The team that was involved in preparing this publication asks Allah ta'ala to bless each and every reader who comes to his word with an open heart and a humble spirit. May the truth he reveals within these pages result in hearts which both experience and produce love, joy, peace, patience, kindness, goodness, faithfulness, gentleness, and self-control in this life and also in the life beyond the grave. To him be all glory for ever and ever.
Amen.

The Good News According to
Luke

Author: Luke, physician and traveling companion of Isa's emissary Paul
Place written: unknown
Date written: probably about A.D. 60-62.

The Holy Scriptures open with the story of creation followed by a description of the first humans enjoying a harmonious relationship with Allah in the beautiful Garden of Eden. This harmony is shattered however when the man and woman rebel against Allah's rule, bringing shame and the curse of death upon themselves. As a result, they are expelled from Paradise (Genesis 2:16-17; 3:1-24). But the story does not end there: through his prophetic messengers Allah promises to send his Messiah (Arabic *al-Masih*, "the anointed one"—a righteous king and savior), who would establish the kingdom of Allah and provide the way for fallen humanity to be restored to a harmonious relationship with the Creator (Genesis 3:15; 12:1-3; 49:10; Deuteronomy 18:18; 2 Samuel 7:10-13; Isaiah 7:14; 9:6-7; 11:1-5; 42:1-9; 52:13–53:12; 61:1-2; Jeremiah 23:5-6; Ezekiel 37:24-28; Micah 5:2).

Each of the first four books of the Injil is an account of the "good news" about how this promised Messiah, Isa al-Masih, came and began to establish Allah's kingdom; but not in the way most people were expecting. In the years just before Isa was born, the Jewish people were suffering under Roman occupation, and were eagerly awaiting deliverance. Because they were Allah's "Chosen People," many of them reasoned that when the Messiah came, he would free them from pagan Roman rule and set up a righteous kingdom in Palestine. But as the accounts of the good news relate, such people, including most religious leaders like the Pharisees, completely missed the point—that Allah's kingdom is not an earthly kingdom established and upheld by military force. Ultimately, it is the reign of Allah in the hearts of his people which is reflected in every aspect of life. Allah was acting to remove the curse of Eden and to free all of humanity (including pagans) not from slavery to Rome, but from slavery to the thoughts, words and deeds which will bring us shame and punishment on the Day of Judgment.

Luke, the author of this account of the good news, was a faithful traveling companion and co-worker of Isa al-Masih's emissary Paul, who remained with Paul even when everyone else had deserted him (2 Timothy 4:9-11); he was also a well-educated medical doctor (Colossians 4:14). Luke was very careful in compiling his data, and diligently researched every account, collecting many eye-witness testimonies, before he composed the most extensive and comprehensive narrative of the life and teachings of Isa al-Masih that we possess (1:1-4).[a] It is likely that Theophilus, a wealthy gentleman, financed

---

a All verse references without an explicit book name refer to Luke.

Luke's research and writing, and oversaw the distribution of the completed work. This was a common practice in the first-century Roman world, and would explain why Luke addressed his account to Theophilus (1:3).

Luke had come to believe that Isa was the promised Messiah. He was probably born into a pagan family and he was writing to a largely non-Hebrew audience, demonstrating that they too could become subjects of Allah's kingdom, regardless of their ethnicity or background (2:29-32; 7:9; 10:25-37; 17:11-19). Hence, Luke emphasizes Isa's compassion for the afflicted, despised, and outcasts of society, including women (7:11-17; 8:1-3, 43-48; 13:10-17), pagans and Samaritans (7:1-10; 17:11-19), tax-collectors and notable sinners (5:27-32; 7:36-50; 19:1-10) and the poor (21:1-4). Luke also emphasizes the importance of prayer (5:16; 6:12, 28; 11:1-13; 18:1-8), and the ministry of Allah's Holy Spirit (1:35, 41, 67; 2:26-27; 4:1, 14, 18; 10:21; 11:13; 12:11-12). He testifies to the joy which the news about Isa brings to those who receive it (2:10; 6:23; 10:20; 19:5-6; 24:52-53). He also records how Isa frequently referred to himself by the Messianic title, "Son of Man" (5:24 with footnote; see also Daniyal/Daniel 7:13-14), who would come "to seek and to save people who are lost" (19:10).

Luke's account is a literary masterpiece, written in the most refined Greek. He begins his narrative with earlier events than the other accounts record, relating prophecies of the births of Prophet Yahya (1:5-25) and of Isa al-Masih (1:26-38). Then he describes Isa's birth in detail, including many events that no one else wrote about (2:1-40). He is also the only author of the Injil who speaks of Isa going up to the temple in al-Quds as a twelve-year old boy (2:41-52). After that, Luke gives the details of the beginning of Isa's public ministry, including his undergoing a ritual washing by Yahya (3:21-22) and his withstanding Shaitan's temptations in the desert (4:1-13).

After telling about the events of Isa's ministry in and around Galilee (4:14–9:50), Luke gives a detailed record of the journey to al-Quds, including much material that is unique to his account (9:51–19:10). He then tells about how, after arriving in al-Quds, Isa died at the hands of the religious and political establishment, who could not accept his claim to be the Messiah (23:26-49), and how, on the third day, he rose again from the dead (24:1-48)! From the beginning, Isa knew that this was his destiny, and that it was necessary to fulfill prophecies (9:21-22, 44; 18:31-33; 24:25-27). Luke ends with an account of the disciples' joy and anticipation as they await the day when Isa would fulfill his promise of sending them Allah's Holy Spirit after he had ascended to his heavenly Father (24:49-53).

Contents

1 Dear Lover of Allah,[a]
Many people have set out to write accounts about the events that occurred
among us. 2 They used the eyewitness reports we possess, those given to us by
the first disciples entrusted with the message. 3 Having carefully investigated
everything from the beginning, I also have written here a careful account
for you, most honorable Theophilus, 4 so you may know with confidence the
truth about everything you were taught.

An Angel Foretells Prophet Yahya's Birth

5 It began like this. When Herod[b] was king of Judea, there was a priest named
Zakariya. He served in the division of Abijah.[c] His wife was Elizabeth, and she
was also a descendant of Harun. 6 Zakariya and Elizabeth were both upright
in Allah's eyes, for they were careful to obey all of the Lord's commandments
and regulations. 7 However, they had no children because Elizabeth was
unable to conceive. And they were both quite old.

8 One day, Zakariya was serving Allah in the temple, for his division was on
duty at that time. 9 He had been chosen by lot (the custom of the priests) to
enter the sanctuary of the Lord's temple to burn incense.[d] 10 At that time of
the incense offering, many members of the community were outside praying.

11 While Zakariya was in the sanctuary, an angel from the Lord appeared
to him, standing to the right of the incense altar. 12 Zakariya was shaken,
overwhelmed with fear at the sight. 13 But the angel said, "Don't be afraid,
Zakariya! Allah has heard your prayer. Your wife, Elizabeth, will give you a son.
You are to name him Yahya. 14 You will be very happy, and many people will
rejoice at his birth, 15 for he will be great in the eyes of the Lord. He will never
drink wine or liquor, but will be filled with Allah's Holy Spirit while still in
his mother's womb. 16 And he will turn many Israelites back to the Lord their
God. 17 He will be a man with the spiritual power of Ilyas,[e] and will precede
the Lord to prepare the people for his arrival. He will turn parents' hearts
toward loving their children, and bring the rebellious to accept wisdom from
the godly."[f]

18 Zakariya said to the angel, "How can I be sure of this? I'm an old man, and
my wife is also well along in years."

---

a 1:1 The Greek name of the original recipient was "Theophilus," or "Lover of Allah." The meaning of that name can be true of anyone today who aspires to live up to it, our highest calling. See Luke 10:25-28.

b 1:5 *Herod*—the reference is to Herod the Great who was ruler of Palestine from 37 to 4 B.C.

c 1:5 *Abijah*—one of the 24 families descended from Harun who were responsible for serving as priests at the temple in al-Quds. The male descendants of these 24 families took turns ministering according to a fixed schedule. See 1 Chronicles 24:1-19.

d 1:9 See Exodus 30:6-8.

e 1:17 *Ilyas*—a prophet (9th century B.C.) who called upon the Israelites to leave their shameful ways and return to Allah (see 1 Kings 17–2 Kings 2).

f 1:17 See Malachi 4:5-6.

19 The angel said to him, "I am Jibrail. I stand in the very presence of Allah, and he sent me to bring you this good news! 20 But now, because you didn't believe what I said, until the child is born you will be silent, unable to speak. For my words will certainly be fulfilled at the appointed time."

21 Meanwhile, the people were waiting for Zakariya to return and wondered why he was taking so long. 22 When he finally came out, he couldn't speak. Then they realized he must have seen a vision in the sanctuary, for he was completely mute, and could only communicate by gesturing.

23 When Zakariya's time of service in the temple was completed, he returned home. 24 Some days later Elizabeth became pregnant and went into seclusion for five months. 25 "The Lord is so gracious!" she exclaimed. "People have disgraced me for being childless. But now Allah has taken away my disgrace!"

An Angel Foretells Isa's Birth

26-27 In the sixth month of Elizabeth's pregnancy, Allah sent the angel Jibrail to a virgin living in Nazareth, a town in Galilee. She was engaged to be married to a man named Yusuf, a descendant of King Dawud, and her name was Maryam. 28 Jibrail appeared to her and said, "Greetings! You have received great favor, for the Lord is with you!"

29 But Maryam was quite shaken, and tried to understand what was meant by this greeting. 30 The angel continued, "Don't be afraid, Maryam, for you have found favor with Allah! 31 So you will conceive and give birth to a son, and you will name him Isa.[g] 32 He will be very great—called the Son of the Most High[h]—and the Lord God will give him the throne of his ancestor Dawud. 33 He will reign over Israel forever, and to his kingdom there will be no end!"

34 Maryam asked the angel, "But how can this happen? I've never been with a man."

35 The angel replied, "The power of the Most High, Allah's Holy Spirit himself, will bring this about. For that reason the baby to be born will be holy and called the Son of the Most High.[i] 36 And even your relative Elizabeth is now pregnant in her old age. People called her barren, but she has conceived a son and is in her sixth month. 37 Nothing is impossible with Allah!"

---

g 1:31 In Hebrew this name would be pronounced "Yeshua" and its meaning is "Yahweh (he who is) saves."

h 1:32 *Son of the Most High*—this phrase absolutely cannot mean that Allah has a son who was conceived in the usual manner. In ancient times among the Israelites the title "Son of the Most High" was applied to kings of Israel (see 2 Samuel 7:14; Zabur/Psalm 2:6-7), but also referred to the promised Messiah, the savior and righteous king from Allah, that is Isa (see John 1:49; 11:27; 20:31). Using the temporal relationship between a loving father and his son the Holy Injil gradually makes known the nature of the eternal relationship between the Most High and al-Masih, revealing that they are one in character and nature (see 10:22; John 5:17-18; 1 John 2:23).

i 1:35 In this verse Isa is called "holy" because he was miraculously born to a virgin mother, and he is called Son of the Most High because he did not have an earthly father and because he was born by the power of Allah's Spirit.

[38] Maryam responded, "I am the Lord's servant. Let this happen to me as you have said." And the angel left her.

Maryam Visits Elizabeth

[39-40] Soon after that, Maryam hurried to the town where Zakariya and Elizabeth lived, located in the hill country of Judea. She entered their house and greeted Elizabeth. [41] When Elizabeth heard Maryam's greeting, Elizabeth's unborn baby leaped in her womb, and Elizabeth was filled with Allah's Holy Spirit.

[42] Elizabeth was thrilled and exclaimed to Maryam, "What a blessed woman you are, and how blessed is your child! [43] Why this honor, that the mother of my Lord should visit me? [44] When I heard your greeting, my baby in my womb jumped for joy. [45] You are blessed because you believed that the Lord God will surely do what he told you."

Maryam Praises Allah

[46] Then Maryam proclaimed,

> "Oh, how my soul praises the Lord,
> [47] how my spirit rejoices in Allah my Savior!
> [48] For he took notice of his lowly servant.[a]
> From now on all generations will say I am blessed.
> [49] For the Mighty One has done great things for me.
> His name is holy!
> [50] He is merciful to all who fear him
> in every generation.[b]
> [51] His powerful arm does mighty things!
> He scatters those who are proud of heart.
> [52] He removes rulers from their thrones,
> but the humble he exalts.
> [53] He supplies the hungry with good things,
> but sends away the rich empty-handed.
> [54] He supports Israel,[c] his servant,
> and treats his people with mercy.
> [55] Just as he promised our ancestors,
> Ibrahim and his children, forever."

[56] So Maryam stayed with Elizabeth about three months and then returned home.

---

a 1:48 See 1 Samuel 1:11; 2:1.

b 1:50 See Zabur/Psalm 103:17.

c 1:54 *He supports Israel*—this addresses Allah's help to the ancient nation. The savior was to rescue his people first of all from their sins. The prophecy has no direct correlation to the relationships between political entities today, 2,000 years later.

Prophet Yahya Is Born

57 The time came for Elizabeth's baby to be born, and she gave birth to a son.
58 Her neighbors and relatives heard how the Lord had been so merciful to
her, and everyone rejoiced with her.

59 When the baby was eight days old, they all came for his circumcision
ceremony.[d] And they wanted to name him after his father, Zakariya. 60 But
Elizabeth said, "No, his name will be Yahya."

61 "Why?" they asked. "None of your relatives has that name!" 62 So they turned
to the baby's father to learn what name he wanted. 63 Zakariya motioned for a
writing tablet, and to their surprise wrote, "His name is Yahya." 64 At that very
moment Zakariya could speak once again, and he was full of praise to Allah.

65 People living in the area were full of awe, and reports of these events
swept through the Judean hill country. 66 And everyone who heard pondered
and asked themselves, "What will the child grow up to be?" For the hand of
the Lord was clearly with him.

Zakariya Praises Allah

67 As for the boy's father, Zakariya was filled with Allah's Holy Spirit and gave
this prophecy:

68 "May the Lord, the God of Israel, be praised![e]
He has come and redeemed his people.
69 He has raised up for us a mighty savior,[f]
through the lineage of his servant Dawud,
70 just as he promised long ago
by his holy prophets—
71 salvation from our enemies
and from the grip of all who hate us.
72 He has shown mercy to our ancestors
by keeping his sacred covenant,
73 the covenant he swore by oath
to our ancestor Ibrahim.
74 Rescued from our enemies,
we will serve Allah without fear,
75 holy and righteous in his sight
every day of our life.

---

d 1:59 According to Allah's command, circumcision was to be performed on the eighth day (see Genesis 17:12).
e 1:68 See Zabur/Psalm 41:13; 72:18; 106:48.
f 1:69 *Mighty savior*—lit. "horn of salvation" (see Zabur/Psalm 18:2). A horn was a symbol of power, authority, and strength (see, for example, literal translations of 1 Samuel 2:10, Jeremiah 48:25; Micah 4:13).

[76] And you, dear child,
will be a prophet of the Most High,
You will precede the Lord to prepare his way.[a]
[77] You will present to his people the understanding of salvation
through forgiveness of their sins.
[78] Because of our God's tender mercy,
the sunrise from heaven[b] will shine upon us.
[79] Giving light to those in the dark shadow of death,[c]
and guiding our steps to the path of peace."

[80] So Yahya grew up and became spiritually strong. And he lived in the wilderness until his public presence in Israel.

Isa al-Masih Is Born

2 Now in those days the ruler, Caesar Augustus,[d] issued a decree that a census
be taken of the entire Roman Empire. [2] This was the first census that took
place when Quirinius was governor of Syria. [3] Residents of the Empire had to
return to their native place to register. [4-5] Yusuf, being a descendant of King
Dawud, had to go to Dawud's home town, Bethlehem in Judea. So he and his fiancée, Maryam, who was pregnant, traveled there from Nazareth in Galilee in order to register.

[6] While they were there, the time came for Maryam to deliver, [7] and she gave
birth to her first child. She wrapped him well in cloths, but because they had no place to stay, she laid him in a manger.

Angels Appear to Shepherds

[8] That night, shepherds were guarding their flocks in the nearby fields.
[9] Suddenly, an angel of the Lord appeared to them, and the glory of the Lord
shone around them. They were terrified. [10] But the angel said, "Don't be afraid!
I announce to you good news, a great joy for everyone! [11] Today, in the town of
Dawud, a savior[e] has been born for you—al-Masih,[f] the Lord! [12] And this is the
proof: you will see the baby, carefully wrapped in cloths, lying in a manger."

[13] Suddenly, the angel was joined by heaven's army in vast array. They all praised Allah, proclaiming,

---

a 1:76 See Isaiah 40:3; Malachi 3:1.

b 1:78 This is a reference to the arrival of the Messiah (compare Numbers 24.17; Isaiah 9:2; 60:1; Malachi 4:2).

c 1:79 See Isaiah 9:2.

d 2:1 Augustus was Roman emperor from 27 B.C. to A.D. 14.

e 2:11 *Savior*—compare Isaiah 43:11; Hosea 13:4.

f 2:11 *al-Masih*—Arabic term derived from the Hebrew *mashiach* which in this context means "The Anointed One," the righteous king, deliverer and savior promised by Allah in the Tawrat, the Zabur, and the Prophets. The usual English form of this word is "Messiah" while the traditional Christian form is "Christ" which comes from the Greek via Latin.

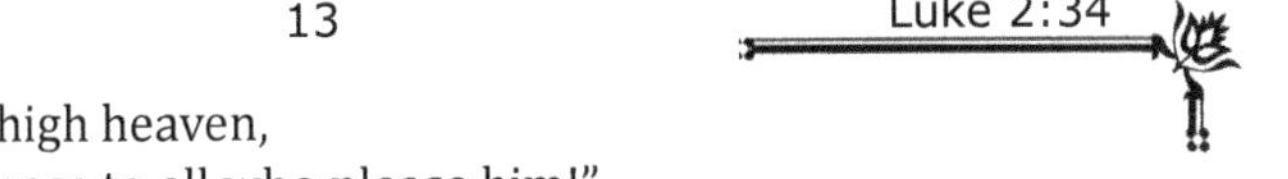

[14] "Glory to Allah in high heaven,
and on earth, peace to all who please him!"

[15] After the angels returned to heaven, the shepherds said, "Let's go to
Bethlehem! Let's see all this the Lord has told us!"
[16] They hurried to the town and found Maryam, Yusuf and the baby, who
was lying in a manger. [17] After seeing him, the shepherds conveyed what the
angel told them about the child. [18] And all who heard the shepherds' story
were astounded. [19] As for Maryam, she treasured and pondered all these
things in her heart. [20] So the shepherds returned to their flocks glorifying and
praising Allah for all they had heard and seen. Everything had happened just
as the angel had said.

Isa Circumcised and Dedicated to the Lord

[21] Eight days later the boy was circumcised and named Isa, according to the
angel's instructions before the child was conceived.
[22] Later came their purification offering, as required by the law of Musa.[g] So
his parents took him to al-Quds[h] to present him to the Lord. [23] For it is written
in the law of the Lord, "Every firstborn male is to be dedicated to the Lord."[i]
[24] And they offered the law's required sacrifice: "a pair of doves or two young
pigeons."[j]

Simeon Prophesies About Isa

[25] At that time a man named Simeon was in al-Quds. He was righteous and
devout, and longed for Allah to rescue Israel. Allah's Holy Spirit was with
him, [26] and had revealed to Simeon that he would not die before he saw the
Lord's promised Messiah. [27] Now the Holy Spirit directed Simeon to enter the
temple, and when Isa's parents came to present him according to the law,
[28] Simeon took the child in his arms and praised Allah, saying,

[29] "Now, Master, let your servant die in peace
as you promised.
[30] For I have seen the salvation
[31] you prepared in the presence of all—
[32] a light for revelation to the nations,
and the glory of your people Israel!"[k]

[33] The child's father and mother were amazed at what was said about him.
[34] Then Simeon blessed them. And to Maryam, the baby's mother, he said,
"This child is appointed for the ruin and restoration of many in Israel. He will

g 2:22 According to the law, a woman was to offer a sacrifice for purification on the fortieth day after giving birth to a son (see Leviticus 12:2-8).
h 2:22 *al-Quds*—also known as "Jerusalem."
i 2:23 See Exodus 13:2, 12, 15.
j 2:24 See Leviticus 12:6-8.
k 2:32 See Isaiah 42:6; 49:6.

be a flashpoint of opposition, 35 exposing the deep recesses of many hearts.
And even your own soul will be pierced with a sword."

Anna Prophesies About Isa

36 Also in the temple was Prophetess Anna, a daughter of Phanuel of the tribe
of Asher. She was very old. She had lived with her husband only seven years
before he died, 37 and then continued on as a widow to her age of eighty-four.[a]
Serving Allah day and night in fasting and prayer, she never left the temple.
38 Happening upon the child there at that time, she thanked Allah and talked
about the child to everyone longing for the deliverance of al-Quds.

39 When Yusuf and Maryam had fulfilled everything the law of the Lord
required, they returned to their own town, Nazareth in Galilee. 40 And the
child grew, became strong, and was very wise. Allah's favor was on him.

The Boy Isa Speaks With Teachers

41 Every year Isa's parents went to al-Quds to celebrate the Passover festival.[b]
42 When he was twelve, they went again, as was customary. 43 After the
festival concluded, they started back home. But the boy Isa remained in al-
Quds, and his parents didn't realize it, 44 thinking he was with their traveling
companions. At the end of their first day's journey they looked for him among
their relatives and friends.

45 When Isa's parents couldn't find him, they returned to al-Quds to search
for him there. 46 On the third day they finally found him in the temple. He
was sitting with the teachers of religion, listening to them and asking them
questions. 47 And all those hearing him were amazed at his understanding
and his comments.

48 But his parents were flabbergasted. "Son," his mother said, "how could
you have done this to us? Your father and I have been in a panic looking for
you!"

49 But Isa said to them, "Why did you search? Didn't you realize that I need
to be in my Father's house?" 50 But they didn't know what he meant.

51 Then he returned with them to Nazareth and remained obedient to them.
And his mother treasured all these things in her heart.

52 And Isa kept growing in wisdom and in stature, and in favor with Allah
and people.[c]

Prophet Yahya Prepares People for Isa

3 In the fifteenth year of the Roman emperor Tiberius' reign, Pontius Pilate
was governor of Judea, Herod was tetrarch of Galilee, his brother Philip

---

a 2:37 Or "She had been a widow for eighty-four years."
b 2:41 *Passover*—this festival was celebrated exclusively in al-Quds in memory of the deliverance of the Israelites from Egyptian slavery under the leadership of Prophet Musa (see Exodus 12; 13:17-22; Deuteronomy 16:1-8).
c 2:52 Compare 1 Samuel 2:26.

was tetrarch of Iturea and Traconitis, Lysanias was tetrarch of Abilene,[d] 2 and
Annas and Caiaphas were the high priests in al-Quds.[e] At that time word
from Allah came to Zakariya's son Yahya, who was living in the wilderness.
3 So Yahya went about preaching in all the Jordan River area, announcing
forgiveness of sins through repentance and a ritual washing. 4 This was as
Isaiah had prophesied in the book he wrote:

"One shouts in the wilderness,
'Prepare the way for the Lord!
Make him a good path!
5 Every valley is to be filled,
every mountain and hill flattened,
the crooked made straight,
and the craggy smooth.
6 And all humanity will see the salvation Allah gives!'"

7 Crowds arrived to undergo ritual washing by Yahya, and he said to them,
"You brood of snakes! Who warned you to flee Allah's impending wrath?
8 Only the fruit of changed lives can prove whether your repentance is real.
And don't comfort yourselves that you are descended from Ibrahim. No, for
I tell you this: Allah can turn the mere stones at our feet into children of
Ibrahim! 9 The ax of judgment is poised, ready to chop the trees at their roots.
Every tree without good fruit will be felled and thrown in the fire."

10 Then the crowds would ask, "What should we do?!"

11 Yahya replied, "If you have two shirts, give one to a person in rags. If you have food, share it with the hungry."

12 Even tax collectors[f] came for ritual washing, asking, "Teacher, what should we do?"

13 He replied, "Take no more in tax than you are required to."

14 And even some soldiers asked, "What should we do?"

Yahya replied, "Don't take money by force or extort anyone. Be content with your wages."

---

d 3:1 *Iturea, Traconitis, Abilene*—today these territories are in Lebanon and Syria.

e 3:1-2 *Tiberius*—Roman emperor from A.D. 14 to 37. *Pontius Pilate*—Roman governor of Judea from A.D. 26 to 36. *Herod*—this is Herod Antipas, son of Herod the Great and the Samaritan woman Malthace. He ruled Galilee and Perea from 4 B.C. to A.D. 39. *Philipp*—Herod Philipp II, the son of Herod the Great and Cleopatra; he ruled from 4 B.C. to A.D. 34. *Lysanias*—his name is found in ancient inscriptions. *Annas*—the high priest from A.D. 6 to 15 but lost the backing of the Romans after that. While many Hebrews continued to recognize Annas, the Romans considered his son-in-law *Caiaphas* to be high priest from A.D. 16 to 36.

f 3:12 *Tax collectors*—hated by the Hebrews for several reasons: they fleeced the people, they worked for the Roman occupiers and they defiled themselves by freely associating with pagans. So "tax collector" was essentially synonymous with "sinner" and "traitor."

15 The people were eagerly expecting the Messiah, and they wondered if Yahya might be the one. 16 He responded to them all with this: "I ritually wash you with water. But the one yet to come is far greater than me. I'm not worthy to even untie his sandals. He will plunge[a] you into Allah's Holy Spirit and into fire.[b] 17 Winnowing fork in hand, he stands ready to clear his threshing floor. He'll gather the grain into his barn, but the chaff will be burned in the everlasting fire." 18 And so, with many other exhortations, Yahya announced the good news to the people.

19 But Yahya criticized Herod for taking his own brother's wife,[c] Herodias, and also for all the other evil things he had done. 20 So Herod added yet another sin to his list—he threw Yahya into prison.

Isa Undergoes Ritual Washing

21 Previous to that, when many people were undergoing ritual washing, Isa himself was washed. And as he prayed heaven opened, 22 and Allah's Holy Spirit, appearing in a form like a dove, descended on him. Then a voice from heaven said, "You are my dear Son! I'm delighted with you!"[d]

The Genealogy of Isa

23 Isa was about thirty years old when he began his public ministry. He was thought to be[e] the son of Yusuf, himself of Heli 24 of Matthat of Levi of Melki of Jannai of Yusuf 25 of Mattathias of Amos of Nahum of Esli of Naggai 26 of Maath of Mattathias of Semein of Josech of Joda 27 of Joanan of Rhesa of Zerubbabel of Shealtiel of Neri 28 of Melki of Addi of Cosam of Elmadam of Er 29 of Joshua of Eliezer of Jorim of Matthat of Levi 30 of Simeon of Judah of Yusuf of Jonam of Eliakim 31 of Melea of Menna of Mattatha of Nathan of Dawud 32 of Jesse of Obed of Boaz of Salmon of Nahshon 33 of Amminadab of Admin of Arni of Hezron of Perez of Judah 34 of Yaqub of Ishaq of Ibrahim of Terah of Nahor 35 of Serug of Reu of Peleg of Eber of Shelah 36 of Cainan of Arphaxad of Shem of Nuh of Lamech 37 of Methuselah of Enoch of Jared of Mahalalel of Kenan 38 of Enosh of Seth of Adam of Allah.

Isa Is Tested by Shaitan

4 Isa, full of Allah's Holy Spirit, left the Jordan River. The Spirit led him into the wilderness, 2 where he was tempted by Iblis for forty days. He ate nothing all that time, and at the end he was very hungry.

---

a 3:16 The Greek word *baptizō* is translated here first as "ritually wash" and then as "plunge." The word means "dip," often of something into water, but also in dye, or, metaphorically, in another substance such as fire.
b 3:16 In the Holy Scriptures, fire is often portrayed as a purifying force (see Zakariya/Zechariah 13:8-9; Malachi 3:1-4; Acts 2:1-4; 1 Corinthians 3:10-15) and also as a manifestation of divine judgement (see Amos 7:4; Zephaniah 1:18; Luke 3:9, 17).
c 3:19 Herod's marriage to his brother's wife was in violation of Allah's law (see Leviticus 18:16; 20:21).
d 3:22 See Genesis 22:2; Zabur/Psalm 2:7; Isaiah 42:1.
e 3:23 *Was thought to be*—that is, he was not the biological son of Yusuf (see 1:30-34).

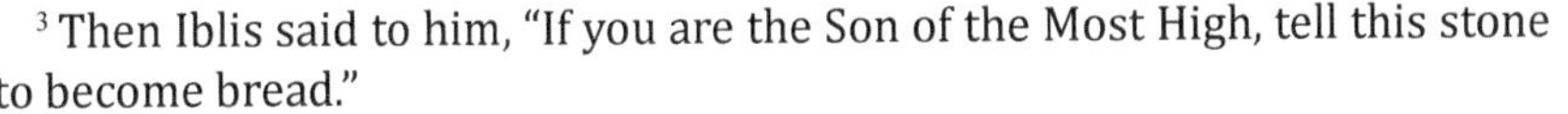

3 Then Iblis said to him, "If you are the Son of the Most High, tell this stone
to become bread."
4 But Isa replied, "It is written in the Scriptures, 'A person cannot live on
bread alone.'"[f]
5 Then Iblis took him to a high spot, flashed before him all the world's
kingdoms, 6 and said, "I can give you authority over all this with all its glory,
for it's mine to offer to whomever I please. 7 It will all be yours if you worship
me."
8 Isa replied, "It is written in the Scriptures,

'You must worship the Lord your God,
and serve only him.'"[g]

9 Then Iblis took him to al-Quds, placed him on the temple's highest point,
and said, "If you are the Son of the Most High, go ahead and jump down. 10 For
it is written in the Scriptures,

'He will command his angels to protect you.'
11 And, 'With their hands they will hold you up,
so you won't even stumble on a stone.'"[h]

12 Isa responded, "The Scriptures also say, 'Do not test the Lord your God.'"[i]
13 So Iblis finished tempting Isa and left him for another time.

Isa Is Rejected at Nazareth

14 Empowered by Allah's Holy Spirit, Isa returned to Galilee. And word about
him spread through the whole region. 15 He taught in the prayer halls and
everyone praised him.
16 And he went to Nazareth where he had grown up. As was his practice, he
entered the prayer hall on the Day of Rest[j] and stood up to read aloud from
the Scriptures. 17 Handed the scroll of Prophet Isaiah, he unrolled it, found
where this was written, and read:

18 "The Spirit of the Lord is with me,
and has anointed[k] me
to announce good news to the poor.
He has sent me to proclaim the release of captives,
sight for the blind,

---

f 4:4 Deuteronomy 8:3.
g 4:8 Deuteronomy 6:13.
h 4:11 Zabur/Psalm 90:11-12.
i 4:12 Deuteronomy 6:16.
j 4:16 *Day of Rest*—according to the law of Musa, every Saturday was to be a sacred day of rest (see Exodus 20:8-11).
k 4:18 *Anointed*—among the ancient Hebrews persons or objects were ritually anointed (rubbed with oil) thus setting them apart for holy service to Allah.

and freedom for the oppressed—
[19] to announce the season of the Lord's favor."

[20] Then he rolled up the scroll, gave it back to the attendant, and sat down.
Every eye in the prayer hall was fixed upon him. [21] Then he addressed them,
saying, "Today, this very Scripture has been fulfilled in your hearing."[a]
[22] Everyone spoke well of him, amazed by the gracious things he was
uttering. And they asked, "Isn't this Yusuf's son?"
[23] Then he said, "You will undoubtedly quote this proverb to me: 'Physician,
heal yourself. The miracles we heard you did in Capernaum, do here in your
home town.' [24] But I tell you the truth," Isa added, "no prophet is welcome in
his hometown.
[25] "The fact is, there were many widows in Israel during Ilyas' time, when
no rain fell for three and a half years and the country endured severe famine.
[26] Yet Allah did not send Ilyas to any of them, but only to a foreign widow of
Zarephath[b] in the land of Sidon.[c] [27] And there were many lepers in Israel during
the time of Prophet Elisha, but none of them were healed, only Naaman the
Syrian."[d]
[28] When the people in the prayer hall heard that, they were all furious.
[29] They jumped up, grabbed Isa, and forced him out of town to the edge of the
cliff on which it was built. They were about to push him over the edge, [30] but
he walked right back through their midst and left.

Isa Casts Out a Demon

[31] Then Isa went to the town of Capernaum in Galilee, and he taught there
weekly on the Day of Rest. [32] His teaching astonished the people, for he spoke
with such authority.
[33] One time in the prayer hall a man possessed by an evil spirit—a demon—
began screaming at Isa, [34] "Ah! What business do you have with us, Isa of
Nazareth? Have you come to destroy us? I know who you are—Allah's Holy
One!"
[35] Isa shot back, "Be quiet and get out of him!" The demon slammed the man
to the ground and left him without a scratch. The people saw it all.
[36] Struck with amazement, they turned to one another, "This man! He
speaks with such power and authority! He even rebukes evil spirits and they
leave!" [37] So news about Isa spread all over the region.

---

a 4:21 Isa is saying he is the Messiah who fulfilled this Scripture. Reading it to his hearers as the Messiah, he is offering them good news: release from slavery to sin, sight in place of spiritual blindness, and freedom from spiritual oppression—all aspects of the Lord's favor.

b 4:26 *Zarephath*—a Phoenician city located in what is now Lebanon. In those days it was an infidel city where people did not acknowledge Allah.

c 4:25-26 See 1 Kings 17.

d 4:27 See 2 Kings 5:1-14.

Isa Heals Many People

38 Leaving the prayer hall, Isa went to Simon's house. Simon's mother-in-law
was suffering with a high fever, and they asked Isa to help her. 39 Standing over
her he rebuked the fever, and it left. And she stood right up and made them
a meal.

40 At sunset, many people brought to Isa loved ones with various ailments.
He placed his hands on each of them and healed every single one. 41 Demons
came out of many others, shouting, "You are the Son of the Most High!" But
Isa rebuked them into silence, because they knew he was the Messiah.[e]

Isa Continues to Preach

42 The next morning Isa went off to an isolated place. But crowds of people
looked for him, found him, and tried to keep him from leaving them. 43 But he
told them, "I must announce the good news of the kingdom of Allah in other
towns, too, because that's why I've been sent." 44 Then he went around Judea
and preached in its prayer halls.

Isa Chooses his First Disciples

5 One day a crowd pressed in on Isa to hear the word of Allah. Being right
next to the Sea of Galilee,[f] 2 he noticed two boats on the shore nearby.
The fishermen had stepped out and were washing their nets, 3 so Isa climbed
into the one owned by Simon and asked him to push it out a bit into the lake.
Sitting down, Isa taught the crowds from there.

4 When he had finished speaking, he said to Simon, "Take it out deeper and
lower your nets for a catch."

5 "Sir," Simon replied, "we worked hard all night long and didn't catch a
thing. But because you tell me, I'll do it." 6 So he and the men with him did just
that, and they caught a huge number of fish—so many that their nets began
to rip. 7 Peter then called his companions in the other boat to come help, and
they filled both boats with fish. In fact, the boats were so loaded down they
were on the verge of sinking.

8 Seeing it all, Simon Peter dropped to his knees before Isa. "Oh, Lord," he
said, "please leave. I'm just a sinful man!" 9 For Simon and the others were
astounded by the quantity of fish they had caught, 10 as were his partners,
Yaqub and John, the sons of Zebedee.

---

e 4:41 The prohibition (not for demons only but also for people—see 8:56) to tell others just who Isa is probably was a result of the widespread misunderstanding of Messianic prophecies. People expected the Messiah to lead a rebellion against the Roman occupation in order to establish the kingdom (see John 6:15). However, his purpose was spiritual deliverance from the chains of sin (see John 8:31-36; 18:36). A second reason is that his God-ordained time had not yet come (see John 7:8). In addition his growing popularity disrupted his ministry (see Mark 1:43-45). Also, Isa did not want people to see him as primarily a miracle-working healer. And of course he did not want to accept the testimony of demons.

f 5:1 *Sea of Galilee*—lit. "Gennesaret."

But Isa said to Simon, "Don't be afraid. From now on you'll fish for people!"
11 And when they brought their boats to shore, they left it all and followed Isa.

Isa Heals a Man With Leprosy

12 When Isa was in a certain town, a man ravaged by leprosy saw him, threw
himself down, and begged to be healed. "Lord," he said, "if you want, you can
heal me."

13 Isa reached out and touched him, saying, "I want to. Be well!" The leprosy
disappeared instantly. 14 Then Isa instructed him not to tell anyone. Instead,
he said, "Show yourself as clean to a priest. Then, as a public testimony, offer
the sacrifice for your cleansing required by the law of Musa."[a]

15 However, word about Isa spread all over, and huge crowds gathered to
hear him preach and be healed of their diseases. 16 But he would often retreat
to the wilderness and pray.

Isa Heals a Paralyzed Man

17 One day while Isa was teaching, Pharisees[b] and teachers of the law of Musa
were attending. They had come from al-Quds and every village in Galilee and
Judea. Now, the Lord's power was with Isa for healing.

18 And some men arrived carrying a paralyzed man on a cot. They hoped to
take him inside and set him in front of Isa. 19 But not finding a way in through
the crowd, they went up on the roof, removed some tiles, and lowered the
man on his cot right down in front of Isa. 20 Seeing their faith, Isa said to the
man, "Your sins are forgiven!"

21 But the scholars of religion and the Pharisees began to wonder, "Who is
this fellow, committing shirk like that! Only Allah himself can forgive sins!"

22 But Isa realized what they were thinking and responded, saying, "Why do
you raise questions in your hearts? 23 What's easier, to simply say 'Your sins
are forgiven,' or to tell this man 'Stand up and walk'? 24 Here's so you'll know
that the Son of Man[c] has authority on earth to forgive sins." Isa then turned
to the paralyzed man and said, "I'm telling you to stand, pick up your cot, and
walk home!"

25 Immediately, in the presence of all, the man stood up, took his cot, and
went home praising Allah. 26 Everyone was stunned. They praised the Most
High, and awestruck exclaimed, "Today, we've witnessed the incredible!"

---

a 5:14 See Leviticus 14:1-32.

b 5:17 *Pharisees*—a religious party which was characterized by their stringent adherence to the laws of the Tawrat, their observance of the customs of their forefathers and their strict attention to matters of ritual purity.

c 5:24 *The Son of Man*—one of the titles of the Messiah, taken from the book of Prophet Daniyal (see Daniyal/Daniel 7:13-14; compare Matthew 26:64). Isa used this title exclusively to refer to himself. In this way Isa implies that he himself is the figure to which Daniyal's prophetic words refer, and that he is the king over all nations, whose kingdom will never end.

Isa Calls Levi

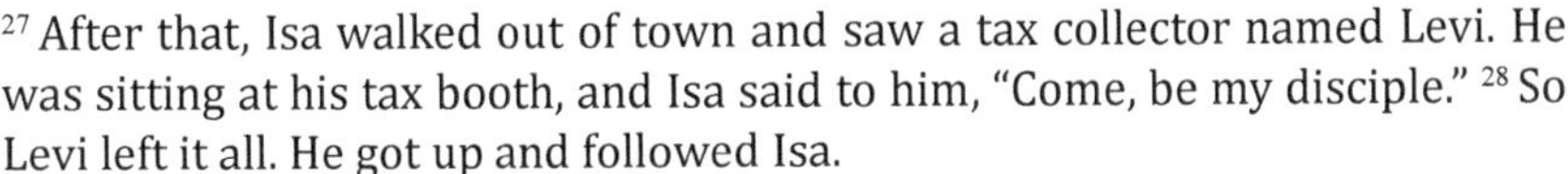

27 After that, Isa walked out of town and saw a tax collector named Levi. He
was sitting at his tax booth, and Isa said to him, "Come, be my disciple." 28 So
Levi left it all. He got up and followed Isa.
29 Levi held a great banquet in his home for Isa, and many guests, including
many tax collectors, attended. 30 But Pharisees and their scholars of religion
complained to Isa's disciples, "Why do you eat and drink with tax collectors
and vile sinners?"
31 Isa answered them, "Healthy people don't need a doctor, only the sick do.
32 And I've not come to call righteous people to repent, only sinners."

Isa Teaches About Fasting

33 One day some people said to Isa, "Yahya's disciples often fast and pray, and
so do the disciples of the Pharisees. But yours stick to their food and drink."
34 Isa responded, "Do you expect a bridegroom's friends to fast when he's
with them?[d] 35 But the time is coming when the groom will be taken away
from them, and in those days they will fast."
36 Then Isa told them an illustration: "No one cuts cloth from a new garment
to patch an old one. That just damages the new without a good match for the
old.
37 "And no one puts new wine into old wineskins. The new bursts the old,
spilling the wine and ruining the skins. 38 New wine must have new wineskins.
39 What's more, those drinking the old don't want the new. They just claim the
old is good enough."

Isa Teaches About the Day of Rest

6 One Day of Rest Isa passed through some grainfields. His disciples plucked
a bit of the grain, rubbed off the husks between their hands, and ate it.
2 But some Pharisees objected, "How can you break the law by harvesting on
a Day of Rest?"[e]
3 Isa replied, "So you haven't read what Dawud did when he and his
companions were hungry? 4 He entered the house of Allah[f] and ate some of
the consecrated bread[g] which was only allowed for priests. And he even gave

---

d 5:34 That is, as long as Isa (the bridegroom) was with his disciples, celebration was in order and fasting would have been inappropriate.

e 6:2 The Hebrews were supposed to leave a part of the harvest for the poor and sojourners. Besides this, the law of Musa allowed people to gather grain in fields belonging to others—this was not considered thievery (see Leviticus 23:22; Deuteronomy 23:25). The Pharisees did not accuse the disciples of Isa of thievery, but of doing work (gathering and threshing grain) on Saturday, the religious Day of Rest.

f 6:4 *House of Allah*—a reference to the tabernacle.

g 6:4 *Consecrated bread*—twelve loaves of bread that were set out every Saturday in the tabernacle, and later in the temple. Bread from the previous week was distributed among the priests (see Exodus 25:30; Leviticus 24:5-9).

some to his companions."[a] [5] Isa concluded, "The Son of Man is the lord of the
Day of Rest."

[6] On another Day of Rest, Isa entered a prayer hall to teach. Among those
attending was a man with a small, paralyzed right hand. [7] The scholars of
religion and Pharisees present sought to indict Isa for lawbreaking. So they
watched him closely to see if he would perform a healing on that holy day.

[8] But Isa knew their plans, so he said to the man with the deformed hand,
"Please come and stand in front of everyone." The man did. [9] Then Isa said to
the religious leaders, "Here's a question for you. What's legal on the Day of
Rest? A good deed? An evil deed? Saving a life, or maybe destroying it?"

[10] He looked around at them all and then said to the man, "Hold out your
hand." He did, and the hand was restored. [11] But the leaders were infuriated,
and they discussed among themselves what to do to Isa.

Isa Chooses Twelve Emissaries

[12] Some days later Isa went up a mountain to pray, and he prayed to Allah
all night long. [13] At dawn he gathered his disciples and designated twelve to
be emissaries: [14] Simon, whom he named Peter, Andrew his brother, Yaqub,
John, Philip, Bartholomew, [15] Matthew, Thomas, Yaqub the son of Alphaeus,
Simon the Zealot,[b] [16] Judas the son of Yaqub, and Judas Iscariot, who ended
up betraying him.

Crowds Follow Isa

[17] Isa descended the mountain with them and stopped on a plain. A large
crowd of his disciples was there, along with great crowds from all over Judea,
al-Quds, and the coastal region of Tyre and Sidon. [18] They had come to hear
him teach and be cured of their diseases. Even those troubled by evil spirits
were healed. [19] So everyone tried to touch him, for he was exuding power and
healing them all.

Isa Reveals Who Is Blessed

[20] Then Isa turned to his disciples and said,

> "Blessed are you who are poor.
> The kingdom of Allah is yours.
> [21] Blessed are you who hunger now.
> You will be satisfied.
> Blessed are you who weep now.
> You will laugh with joy.

[22] Blessed are you when, because you follow the Son of Man, people hate you,
ostracize you, insult you, or curse you as evil. [23] When that happens, rejoice!

---

a 6:3-4 See Leviticus 24:8-9; 1 Samuel 21:1-6.

b 6:15 *Zealot*—member of an extreme religious-political movement which rose up against the Roman occupation of Israel.

Leap for joy! For a great reward awaits you in heaven! Those were the same things their ancestors did to the prophets.

Isa Reveals Who Will Have Trouble

24 "Woe to you who are rich.
You've now received all you'll get.
25 Woe to you who are well-fed now.
Hunger is on its way.
Woe to you who live gaily now.
You'll come to mourn and weep.
26 Woe to you praised by society.
That's how its ancestors treated false prophets.

Isa Teaches Love for One's Enemies

27 "But for you willing to listen, I say,

Love your enemies.
Do good to those who hate you.
28 Bless those who curse you.
Pray for those who mistreat you.
29 When you're slapped on one cheek,
offer the other too.
When your coat is taken,
don't withhold your shirt.
30 Give to all who ask.
And when what's yours is seized,
don't demand it back.
31 Treat people
as you want to be treated.

32 "So, if you love only those who love you, what credit is that to you? Even
vile sinners love those who love them.
33 And if you're good to those good
to you, what credit is that? Even vile sinners do the same.
34 And if you lend
money to those who'll repay you, what credit is that to you? Even vile sinners
lend to their own kind if they'll receive it back.
35 "Instead, love your enemies. Do good. Lend without expecting repayment.
The rewards will be huge, and you'll be children of the Most High—the One
who is kind to the ungrateful and wicked.
36 Be compassionate, just like your
Father.

Isa Teaches Not to Judge Others

37 "Don't judge others, and you won't be judged. Don't condemn others, and
you won't be condemned. Forgive others, and you'll be forgiven.
38 Give, and
you'll be given to—a basketful, pressed down, shaken to make room for

more, overflowing into your lap. For the amount you are given depends on the amount you give out."

[39] Then Isa used illustrations. "Can one blind person lead another? Won't they both fall into a hole? [40] Students aren't better than their teacher. But when fully trained, they equal their teacher.

[41] "And how is it you can see a speck in your friend's eye when you don't notice a log in your own? [42] How can you even imagine saying to your friend, 'Let me take that speck out of your eye,' when a log sits in your own? You hypocrite. First pull the log from your own eye. Then you'll see clearly enough to remove your friend's speck.

Isa Teaches About Good Deeds

[43] "A good tree doesn't produce bad fruit, nor a bad tree good fruit. [44] Every tree is identified by its fruit. Figs are not gathered from thornbushes, nor grapes picked from brambles. [45] A good person from the richness of a good heart does good. An evil person from an evil heart does evil. Conduct is the outflow of the heart.

Isa Teaches About a Well-Founded Life

[46] "Why call me 'dear Lord' if you don't do what I say? [47] Let me tell you what someone is like who comes to me, listens to my teaching, and obeys it. [48] That person is like a man who builds a solid house. He digs deep and lays its foundation on bedrock. Then, when a flood rages and its waters slam against the house, they can't budge it, because it's so well built. [49] But anyone who listens to my teaching and doesn't obey it is like a man who builds a house with no foundation, right on the topsoil. When floodwaters slam against that house, it quickly collapses, totally ruined."

A Roman Officer Believes in Isa

7 When Isa finished saying all this to the people, he returned to Capernaum. [2] A Roman centurion there had a servant he valued highly, but the servant became sick and was near death. [3] So when that officer heard about Isa, he sent some Hebrew elders with the request that Isa come and heal the servant. [4] When the elders arrived, they pleaded with Isa, testifying of the officer, "He's worthy of your aid, [5] for he loves our people and built a prayer hall for us."

[6] So Isa went with them. But just before they arrived at the house, the centurion sent some friends with a message: "Lord, don't trouble yourself by coming to my home. I'm not worthy of the honor. [7] I'm not even worthy to meet you. Just say the word, and my servant will be healed. [8] For I understand authority, being under my superiors but over my soldiers. I tell one to go, another to come, and my servant to do this or that, and they obey."

[9] Amazed, Isa turned to the crowd following him and said, "Well! I haven't seen faith like this anywhere in Israel!" [10] And when the officer's friends returned to his house, they found the slave was well.

Isa Brings a Widow's Son Back to Life

11 Soon afterward Isa went to the town of Nain. His disciples and a large crowd
followed. 12 As he approached the town gate, a body was being carried out for
burial—that of a widow's only son. And a large crowd from the town was with
her. 13 The Lord saw the widow and felt deeply compassionate for her. "Don't
cry!" he said. 14 Then he approached the funeral pallet and put his hand on it.
The pallbearers stopped. "Young man," he said, "I tell you, get up!" 15 Then the
dead boy sat up and began to talk.[a] And Isa handed him to his mother.

16 The crowd, shaken with awe, praised Allah, saying "A mighty prophet
is among us!" and "Allah has come and helped his people!" 17 And the news
spread throughout Judea and all the surrounding region.

Isa Teaches About Prophet Yahya

18 Yahya's disciples told Yahya about all of this. Then he called 19 and sent two
of them to the Lord with this question: "Are you the one promised to come,[b]
or should we expect someone else?"

20 So the two men from Yahya arrived and said to Isa, "Yahya the Baptizer[c]
sent us to ask, 'Are you the one promised to come, or should we expect
someone else?'"

21 Then and there Isa cured many people of diseases, afflictions, and evil
spirits, and he restored sight to many who'd been blind. 22 Then he told
Yahya's disciples, "Go and report to Yahya what you've seen and heard—blind
people see, lame walk, lepers are healed, deaf hear, dead are brought back to
life, and the poor are given the good news.[d] 23 And also this: 'Blessed are those
not offended by me.'"[e]

24 After Yahya's disciples left, Isa spoke about Yahya to the crowds. "Why
did you go into the wilderness—to watch some reeds blow in the wind? No.
25 Or did you go to see a man dressed in fine clothes? No. People who wear
beautiful clothes and live in luxury stay in palaces. 26 So, you went to see a
prophet, right? But he is even more than a prophet. 27 Yahya is the messenger
about whom the Scriptures speak,

> 'I am sending my messenger ahead of you.
>   He will prepare your way in front of you.'[f]

---

a 7:15 Compare 1 Kings 17:23.
b 7:19 *The one promised to come*—a reference to the long-awaited Messiah.
c 7:20 *Baptizer*—the ritual washings that Prophet Yahya performed (e.g., 7:29-30) are also known as "baptisms," from a form of the Greek word used here.
d 7:22 See Isaiah 29:18; 35:5-6; 61:1.
e 7:23 Apparently Prophet Yahya, like everyone else, expected a more political type of Messiah with a more proactive approach to social evil. Instead, he was thrown into prison for telling the truth about Herod, and Isa did nothing about it! In light of these realities it is easy to see why Yahya began to have doubts about Isa and even to be upset with him.
f 7:27 Malachi 3:1.

28 I'm telling you, of all mortals,[a] Yahya is the greatest. Yet even the kingdom of
Allah's least is greater than him!"[b]

29 When the crowds heard this, the tax collectors with them, they all agreed
that Allah's ways were right. Now, they had been ritually washed by Yahya.
30 But the Pharisees and scholars of religious law, having refused to be washed
by Yahya, had rejected Allah's will for themselves.

31 Then Isa asked, "The people of this generation—what can I compare them
to? What are they like? 32 They're like children, whining in the public square,

'We played the flute,
  but you wouldn't dance.
We sang sad songs,
  but you wouldn't cry.'

33 For Yahya the Baptizer has come and performed ritual washings, but since
he doesn't eat bread or drink wine, you say, 'He's possessed by a demon!'
34 The Son of Man has come too. He eats and drinks, but you say of him, 'Ah!
A glutton and a drunkard! A friend of tax collectors and sinners!' 35 But true
wisdom is evident in all the lives of its followers."

Isa Is Anointed by a Sinful Woman

36 A Pharisee invited Isa to dinner, so he entered the man's home and sat at the
table. 37 And an immoral woman from town heard Isa was there. So she took
an alabaster jar of perfume, 38 went behind him at his feet, and wept. Her tears
fell on his feet, and she wiped them with her hair. She kept kissing them, and
then rubbed them with the perfume.

39 Observing all this, the Pharisee who had invited Isa said to himself, "If
this man were a prophet, he would know what kind of woman is touching
him—a sinner!"

40 Then Isa responded to his host. "Simon, I have something to say to you."

"Go ahead, teacher," he replied.

41 Isa said, "Two people owed a creditor money, one 500 denarii[c] and the
other 50. 42 Neither of them could repay him, but he canceled both their debts.
Which of the two debtors loved the man more?"

43 Simon answered, "I suppose the one with the larger debt."

"You answered well," Isa said. 44 Then he turned to the woman and said
to Simon, "Look at this woman. When I entered your home, you didn't offer
me water for my feet, but she has washed them with her tears and dried
them with her hair. 45 You didn't greet me with a kiss. But she, from the time I

---

a 7:28 *Of all mortals*—lit. "among those born of a woman."

b 7:28 Yahya fulfilled an important role in announcing the coming of the Messiah, but even the least important follower of Isa has a huge advantage over all people who lived before his coming, even the greatest of them.

c 7:41 A denarius was a Roman coin, about equal to a day's wage for a hired laborer (see Matthew 20:2)

entered, has not stopped kissing my feet. [46] You didn't bless me with oil for my head. But she has anointed my feet with perfume.

[47] "So let me tell you, her many sins have been forgiven, as shown by her great love. But a person forgiven of little loves little." [48] Then Isa said to the woman, "Yes, your sins are forgiven."

[49] The men at the table said among themselves, "Who is this fellow, that he even forgives sin?"

[50] And Isa said to the woman, "Your faith has saved you. Go in peace."

Women Follow Isa

8 After that, Isa went from one town and village to another announcing the good news about the kingdom of Allah. His twelve emissaries were with him, [2] and also some women he'd cured of evil spirits and diseases—Maryam from Magdala, from whom he cast out seven demons; [3] Joanna, the wife of Chuza, an official of Herod; Susanna; and many others who were contributing from their own resources to the support of Isa and his disciples.

A Parable About a Farmer Planting Seed

[4] One day a large crowd gathered, people having come from town after town. And he taught them with a parable: [5] "A farmer went out to plant his seed. As he scattered it across his field, some fell on a path. It was stepped on, and birds ate it. [6] Other seed fell among rocks. It started to grow, but lacking moisture it dried up. [7] Other seed fell among thorns. They grew up with it and choked it out. [8] And other seed fell on rich soil. It grew and produced a crop a hundred times as great." He concluded by saying loudly: "Whoever has ears should use them to listen!"

[9] Isa's disciples asked him what the parable meant, [10] and he replied, "You've been given access to the secrets of the kingdom of Allah. But others get parables, so:

> 'They look but don't see.
>   They hear but don't understand.'[d]

[11] "Here's what the parable means. The seed is Allah's word. [12] The seeds on the path are those who hear the message, but then Iblis comes along and snatches it from their hearts so they won't believe and be saved.[e] [13] The seeds on rocky soil are those who hear the message and joyfully accept it. But since they don't have deep roots, they believe for only a while, and when difficulty arises they fall away. [14] The seeds that fell among thorns are those

d 8:10 Isaiah 6:9. By encoding his teaching in parables, Isa ensures that those who approach spiritual issues half-heartedly will remain in the dark, while truth seekers, who apply themselves diligently to understand his teaching, eventually will be rewarded.

e 8:12 *Saved*—from the flames of hell (see Jude 1:23), from the anger of Allah and his judgments (see Romans 5:9), from an empty life (see 1 Peter 1:18), from sin (see Matthew 1:21), and from Iblis (see 2 Timothy 2:26).

who hear the message, but earthly concerns, wealth, and pleasures arise to
choke the plants, and they don't mature. 15 Finally, the seeds on the rich soil
are those who, with a good and sincere heart hear the message, embrace it,
and patiently produce a harvest.

A Parable About a Lamp

16 "No one lights a lamp only to cover it with a bowl or stash it under a bed.
We put it up on a stand to light the way for those inside. 17 Everything hidden
will eventually be evident; everything concealed will be brought to light and
made known.

18 "So pay attention to how you listen. Those who hold to truth will be given
more. But those who don't, even what they think they possess will be taken
away."

Isa Teaches About His Real Family

19 After that, Isa's mother and brothers came to see him, but they couldn't get
to him because of the crowd. 20 People told Isa, "Your mother and brothers are
standing outside and want to see you."

21 But Isa replied to them, "My mother and brothers are those who hear
Allah's word and obey it."

Isa Calms a Storm

22 One day Isa and his disciples got into a boat, and he said to them, "Let's go to
the other side of the lake." So they started out. 23 As they sailed, Isa fell asleep.
But then a fierce storm blew down on the lake, the boat was filling with water,
and they were in danger.

24 The disciples went and woke Isa, shouting, "Master, Master, we're
drowning!"

Isa woke up and rebuked the wind and the waves. The storm stopped
immediately, and everything was calm. 25 Then he asked them, "Where is your
faith?"

Frightened and amazed, the disciples asked each other, "Who is this? Even
wind and waves obey his commands!"

Isa Heals a Demon-Possessed Man

26 After sailing on they landed in the region of the Gerasenes, across the lake
from Galilee. 27 As Isa was getting out on shore, he was met by a man who
formerly lived in town, but was now possessed by demons. Homeless and
naked, for a long time he had stayed among the local tombs.

28 Seeing Isa he shrieked, fell down in front of him, and screamed, "What
business do you have with me, Isa, Son of the Most High God? Please don't
torment me!" 29-30 For the spirit had often taken control of the man, so that
even when he was under guard and in chains and shackles, he simply broke
his bonds and was driven by the demon into the wilderness.

Isa commanded the evil spirit to come out of the man, demanding, "What is your name?"

"Legion,"[a] it replied, for many demons had entered him, 31 and they begged Isa not to send them into the abyss of hell.

32 There happened to be a large herd of pigs feeding on a nearby hill, and the demons begged Isa to let them enter the pigs.

So he let them. 33 The demons went out of the man and entered the pigs, and the entire herd rushed down the hill into the lake and drowned.

34 The herdsmen saw all this and fled, reporting the news in the town and countryside. 35 People came out to see what had happened, and they went up to Isa. There they saw the man from whom the demons had left. He was sitting at Isa's feet, clothed and sane. They became frightened. 36 Then those who'd witnessed the events told how the demon-possessed man had been set free, 37 and all the people from the Gerasene region, seized with fear, begged Isa to leave.

So he got into the boat and crossed back to the other side. 38 But before he started off, the man from whom the demons had gone out pleaded to go with him. Instead, Isa sent him off, saying, 39 "Return to your family and tell them all Allah did for you." So he went throughout the town declaring what Isa had done for him.

Isa Heals in Response to Faith

40 After the crossing, the crowd welcomed Isa, having waited for his return. 41 Then a man named Jairus, leader of the prayer hall, threw himself at Isa's feet and begged him to go to his home. 42 Jairus' only child, a daughter about twelve years old, was dying.

Isa went with him, surrounded by the crowds. 43 Now, a woman was there who had suffered for twelve years from chronic bleeding. She had exhausted her resources on doctors, but no one could cure her. 44 Coming up behind Isa, she touched the fringe of his cloak.[b] Immediately, her bleeding stopped.

45 "Who touched me?" Isa asked.

Everyone denied it, and Peter said, "Master, whole crowds surround and jostle you!"

46 But Isa said, "Someone deliberately touched me. I felt power leave me." 47 The woman realized she couldn't go unnoticed. So she went and fell to her knees, trembling, in front of Isa. Then, with the people listening, she explained why she had touched him and how she had been immediately healed. 48 "Daughter," he said, "your faith has healed you. Go in peace."

49 Just as he spoke to her, a messenger arrived from the home of the prayer hall leader. The man told Jairus, "Your daughter has died, so you needn't trouble the teacher any further."

---

a 8:29-30 A legion was a division of the Roman army consisting of about 6,000 men.

b 8:44 Tassels were sewn with blue cords onto the fringes of men's clothing. These tassels were to remind the Hebrews that they must fulfill all of the laws of Allah (see Numbers 15:38-40; Deuteronomy 22:12).

[50] But when Isa heard what happened, he told Jairus, "Don't be afraid. Just
have faith, and she will be healed."
[51] When they arrived at the house, Isa didn't allow anyone in with him
except Peter, John, Yaqub, and the young girl's father and mother. [52] Everyone
inside was weeping and wailing, but he said, "Don't weep. She isn't dead, only
sleeping."
[53] Knowing she was dead, the crowd laughed at him. [54] But Isa held her hand
and said in a loud voice, "Child, get up!" [55] Her life returned, and she got up
immediately. Then Isa told them to give her something to eat. [56] Her parents
were overwhelmed with amazement, but Isa ordered them not to tell anyone
what happened.

Isa Sends Out His Twelve Emissaries

9 One day Isa called together his twelve emissaries and gave them the power
and authority to cast out all demons and to heal all diseases. [2] Then he
sent them out to proclaim the kingdom of Allah and to heal the sick. [3] And he
added these instructions: "Don't take anything on the journey—not a walking
stick, a pack, food, money, or a second shirt. [4] Wherever you go, stay in the
same house until you depart. [5] And whatever places refuse you welcome,
when you leave shake their dust from your feet as a testimony against them."[a]
[6] So they set off and went from village to village, announcing the good news
and healing all the sick.

King Herod Is Confused

[7] Herod the tetrarch[b] heard about all this and was puzzled. Some were saying
Yahya had come back to life. [8] Others thought Isa was Ilyas or another prophet
of old who'd come back to life.
[9] But Herod said, "I beheaded Yahya, so who's this man I hear so much
about?" And he was eager to see him.

Isa Feeds Five Thousand People

[10] When the emissaries returned, they reported to Isa everything they'd done.
Then he slipped quietly away with them to the town of Bethsaida. [11] But the
crowds found out and followed him. So he welcomed them and taught them
about the kingdom of Allah, and he healed those who were sick.
[12] Late that afternoon the twelve emissaries approached Isa and said, "Send
the crowd away. Then they can go to the nearby villages and farms to find
food and lodging. The place we're in is so desolate!"
[13] But Isa said, "You feed them."

---

a 9:5 Devout Hebrews shook the dust from their feet when they returned from another country, as if they were ritually cleansing themselves from defilement. Doing that after contact with other Hebrews would be equal to calling them pagans.

b 9:7 The reference is to Herod Antipas (see footnote on 3:1).

"We have only five loaves of bread and two fish!" they answered. "Or are we to go and buy food for this whole crowd?!" [14] Now, the number of men alone came to about 5,000.

Isa said to his disciples, "Tell the people to sit in groups of about fifty." [15] They did so, and everyone sat down. [16] Then Isa took the five loaves and two fish, looked up to heaven, blessed the food, broke it into pieces, and kept handing it to the disciples for distribution to the people. [17] And everyone ate their fill. Afterward, the disciples picked up the leftover pieces, which filled twelve baskets.

Peter Declares That Isa Is the Messiah

[18] One day Isa was praying by himself. His disciples were with him, and he asked them, "Who do people say I am?"

[19] They replied, "Some say Yahya the Baptizer, some Ilyas, and others that you're a prophet of old come back to life."

[20] Then he asked them, "And who do you say I am?"

Peter answered, "You are the Messiah[c] sent by Allah."

Isa Predicts His Death

[21] Isa strictly warned his disciples not to tell anyone.[d] [22] "The Son of Man must suffer many things," he said, "and be rejected by the elders, the head priests, and the scholars of religion. And he will be killed, but on the third day he will come back to life."

[23] Then he spoke to everyone, saying, "Anyone who wants to be my disciple must set their own self aside, take up their cross daily,[e] and follow me. [24] Whoever wants to keep their life will lose it. But whoever gives up their life for my sake will save it. [25] What does anyone gain by winning the whole world if they lose or forfeit their life? [26] Whoever is ashamed of me and my teaching, the Son of Man will be ashamed of them when he comes back—returning in all his glory, with the glory of the Father and the holy angels. [27] And I tell you

---

c 9:20 *Messiah*—righteous king and deliverer promised by Allah in the Tawrat, the Zabur, and the Prophets. The term comes from the Hebrew *mashiach* which means "anointed one," a reference to the use of holy anointing oil in the installation ceremonies for priests and kings (e.g., 1 Samuel 10:1). This term went into Arabic as *al-Masih* and into Greek as *Christos* from which the English *Christ* is derived.

d 9:21 The Hebrews incorrectly thought that their Messiah must free them from foreign domination, and so were eager to declare Isa their king, hoping he lead an anti-Roman liberation movement (see John 6:15; Acts 1:6). But Isa al-Masih's purpose was the saving of souls, freeing humanity from slavery to sin (see Romans 6:17-23; 8:2).

e 9:23 To take up one's cross is to put one's own agenda to death and to live for Allah's agenda. This can involve taking on shame and sometimes even physical harm from those who do not understand.

the truth, some people standing right here will not die before they see the kingdom of Allah."[a]

Isa Is Transfigured

[28] About eight days after saying those things, Isa took Peter, John, and Yaqub up a mountain to pray. [29] And as he was praying, his face changed and his clothes became dazzling white. [30] And suddenly, two men appeared—Musa and Ilyas—talking with Isa. [31] All in glorious splendor, they discussed his earthly departure which he was soon to bring about in al-Quds.

[32] Meanwhile, Peter and his companions had been overcome by sleep. Upon waking, they saw Isa in glory and the two standing with him. [33] As Musa and Ilyas were about to leave, Peter, hardly knowing what he was doing, burst out saying, "Master, it's so good we're here! Should we put up three shelters—one each for you, Musa, and Ilyas?" [34] As he was speaking a cloud overshadowed and then enveloped them. They were terrified.

[35] Then, from the cloud a voice spoke: "This is my Son, my Chosen! Listen to him!"[b] [36] When the voice finished, Isa was there alone. In the days that followed, his disciples were silent about all this, not telling anyone what they had seen.

Isa Heals a Demon-Possessed Boy

[37] The next day, when they came down the mountain, a large crowd met Isa. [38] And a man in the crowd called out to him, "Teacher, I beg you to see my son, my only child. [39] For an evil spirit keeps seizing him. My son suddenly screams, is thrown into convulsions, and foams at the mouth. The spirit beats him terribly and seldom leaves. [40] I begged your disciples to cast it out, but they couldn't."

[41] Isa responded, "Yours is a faithless and twisted generation. How long do I have to stay and put up with you?" To the man he said, "Bring your son here."

[42] As the boy came forward, the demon threw him down and into a convulsion. But Isa rebuked the evil spirit, healed the boy, and gave him back to his father. [43] And the people were awestruck at the power of Allah.

Isa Again Predicts His Death

When everyone was marveling at all he had done, Isa said to his disciples, [44] "Listen carefully to me here. The Son of Man will be handed over to his

---

a 9:27 Many commentators believe that the following nine verses explain these words of Isa (see also John 1:14; 2 Peter 1:16). Others believe that Isa spoke about the powerful impact of Allah's kingdom in human hearts as evidenced by the growing number of his followers and the spread of the good news after his resurrection. There are also other interpretations.

b 9:35 The wording here comes from ancient prophecies (Deuteronomy 18:15; Zabur/Psalm 2:7; Isaiah 42:1). Allah's voice from heaven thus asserts that Isa is the fulfillment of these prophecies: he is the prophet promised by Prophet Musa, the Messiah, and Isaiah's "Servant of the Lord."

enemies." [45] But they didn't know what he was talking about. It was all a blur
to them. They couldn't figure it out, and they were afraid to ask him about it.

Isa Reveals Who Are the Greatest in Allah's Kingdom

[46] Then his disciples started to argue about which of them was the greatest.
[47] But Isa, knowing their thoughts, stood a child at his side. [48] Then he said
to them, "Whoever for my sake welcomes a child also welcomes me. And
whoever welcomes me also welcomes the One who sent me. The least among
you is the greatest."

Isa Teaches About Using His Name

[49] To that John said, "Master, we saw someone use your name to cast out
demons, and we hindered him because he wasn't one of us."
[50] But Isa said, "Don't do that. Anyone not against you is for you."

Samaritans Oppose Isa

[51] As the time for his ascension to heaven drew near, Isa set about with
determination to head to al-Quds. [52] Along the way, he sent people on to a
Samaritan village to prepare for his arrival. [53] But because his destination was
al-Quds, the village wouldn't welcome him.[c] [54] When Yaqub and John heard
that, they said to Isa, "Lord, should we call down fire from heaven and destroy
them?"[d] [55] But Isa turned to them with a rebuke, [56] and they all proceeded to
another village.

Following Isa Is Costly

[57] As they were on the way, someone said to Isa, "I'll follow you wherever you
go."
[58] But Isa warned, "Foxes have dens, and birds have nests, but the Son of
Man has no place to lay his head."
[59] To another he said, "Follow me."
The man deferred, saying, "Lord, let me go be with my father until he dies."
[60] But Isa told him, "Let the spiritually dead bury their own dead. You're to
go and proclaim the kingdom of Allah."
[61] Still another said, "I'll follow you, Lord, but first let me go and say good-
bye to my family."
[62] But Isa warned, "Anyone who sets out to plow by looking back is not
suited for the kingdom of Allah."

Isa Sends Out His Disciples

10 After that the Lord chose seventy-two others, sending them ahead in
pairs to all the towns and places he planned to go. [2] And he said to
them, "The harvest is vast, but there are few workers. So pray to the Lord, the
head of the harvest, to put more workers into his fields. [3] Listen, I'm sending

---

c 9:53 There was a long history of animosity between the Samaritans and the Hebrews.
d 9:54 Compare 2 Kings 1:10-12.

you out like lambs among wolves. 4 Don't take money with you, or a pack, or an extra pair of sandals. And don't stop for greetings on the way.

5 "Whenever you enter a house, say, 'Allah's peace to this home.' 6 If the people are peace-loving, your blessing will remain. If they are not, it will return to you. 7 Don't move from house to house, but stay in one, eating and drinking what they provide. Workers deserve their wages.

8 "When you enter a town and it welcomes you, eat whatever is set before you. 9 Heal its sick, and tell them, 'The kingdom of Allah has come to you!' 10 But when you enter a town and it refuses to welcome you, go out into its streets and say, 11 'Against you we wipe off even your town's dust from our feet.[a] But know this, the kingdom of Allah has come to you!' 12 I assure you, on the Day of Judgment even Sodom[b] will be better off than that town.

13 "Woe to you, Korazin and Bethsaida! For if the miracles I did in you had been done in Tyre and Sidon, they would have repented long ago, grieving in sackcloth and ashes. 14 So Tyre and Sidon will be better off in the Judgment than you. 15 And you, Capernaum, will not be raised to heaven. You'll descend to hell."[c]

16 Then he said to his disciples, "Anyone who listens to you is listening to me. But anyone who rejects you is rejecting me. And anyone who rejects me is rejecting the One who sent me."

17 When the seventy-two disciples returned, they joyfully reported, "Lord, even demons obey us when we use your name!"

18 "I was watching Shaitan fall like lightning from heaven! 19 Listen, I've given you authority to trample snakes and scorpions—authority over all the power of the enemy. Nothing will harm you. 20 However, don't rejoice because evil spirits obey you. Rejoice because your names are written in heaven."

Isa Teaches About Who Knows Allah

21 At that moment Isa was filled with joy in Allah's Holy Spirit, and he said, "I praise you, Father, Lord of heaven and earth, for hiding these things from those considered so wise and understanding, and for revealing them instead to the childlike. Yes, Father, doing it this way pleased you."

22 Isa continued, "My Father entrusted everything to me. No one knows the Son except the Father, or the Father except the Son—and anyone to whom the Son chooses to reveal him."

23 And turning to his disciples, he said to them privately, "Blessed are you to have seen these things! 24 I tell you this, many prophets and kings longed to see what you see, but did not. And they longed to hear what you hear, but did not."

Isa Reveals the Most Important Commandment

25 Once, a scholar of religious law wanting to test Isa stood up and asked him, "Teacher, what must I do to inherit eternal life?"

---

a 10:11 See footnote on 9:5.

b 10:12 See Genesis 19:1-29.

c 10:15 See Isaiah 14:13, 15.

26 Isa replied, "What's written in the law? How do you see it?"
27 The man answered, "'Love the Lord your God with all your heart and all
your soul and all your strength and all your mind.'[d] Also, 'Love your neighbor
as yourself.'"[e]
28 "You answered well," Isa told him. "Do that and you'll live."
29 But the man wanted to vindicate himself, so he asked Isa, "And who is my
neighbor?"

A Parable About a Good Samaritan

30 Isa replied with this: "A man traveling down from al-Quds to Jericho was
attacked by bandits. They stripped him, beat him, and left him half dead.
31 "By chance a priest was going down the same road. But when he saw the
man, he passed by on the other side. 32 A Levite[f] also went down that way, saw
the man, and also passed by on the other side.
33 "Then a mere Samaritan[g] came traveling along. He saw the man and felt
compassion for him. 34 So he went over, dressed the man's wounds with wine
and oil, and bandaged them. Then he put the man on his own donkey and
brought him to an inn and cared for him. 35 The next day he took out two silver
coins[h] and handed them to the innkeeper, saying, 'Take care of him. And if you
spend any more than this, I'll pay you when I return.'"
36 Then Isa asked, "Which of the three would you say was a neighbor to the
man attacked by bandits?"
37 The scholar replied, "The one who showed him mercy."
Then Isa said to him, "So go and do the same."

Isa Visits Martha and Maryam

38 As Isa and the disciples traveled on, he entered a certain village where
a woman named Martha welcomed him into her home. 39 She had a sister,
Maryam, who sat at the Lord's feet, listening to what he taught. 40 But Martha
was very busy with all her preparations. So she approached Isa and said,
"Lord, don't you care that my sister has left me to do all the work myself? Tell
her to help me."
41 But the Lord said to her, "Dear Martha, you're anxious and upset over so
many things. 42 Only one thing is necessary. Maryam chose what's best, and it
won't be taken from her."

---

d 10:27 Deuteronomy 6:5.
e 10:27 Leviticus 19:18.
f 10:32 *Levite*—the Levites were one of the twelve tribes of the Israelite nation. Allah chose the Levites to be the priests' assistants.
g 10:33 *Samaritan*—the Samaritans are a people of mixed origin, descendants of the ten northern tribes of Israel together with immigrants from other parts of the Assyrian Empire. They believe in the Tawrat, but not the other books of the Scriptures. There was long-standing animosity between the Samaritans and the Hebrews.
h 10:35 *Two silver coins*—lit. "two denarii." This was two day's pay for a common laborer.

Isa Teaches About Prayer

11 Once, after Isa finished praying, one of his disciples asked him, "Lord,
teach us to pray—like Yahya, who taught his disciples to pray."
2 Isa said, "When you pray, say:

Father, may your name be kept holy.
    May your kingdom come.
3 Give us every day the food we need.
4 Forgive us of our sins,
    as we forgive all who sin against us.
And don't bring us into trying times."

5 Then he told them this: "Suppose it's midnight, and you go to a friend's
place nearby. You tell him, 'Please give me three loaves of bread. 6 A friend on
a trip just showed up, and I've got nothing to feed him!' 7 But the friend you
approached responds from inside, 'Don't bother me. The door's bolted. My
kids and I are all in bed. I can't get up to help you.' 8 Let me tell you, though he
may not help simply because he's your friend, if you keep asking, your bold
persistence will rouse him to give you whatever you need.
9 "And so I tell you, keep asking and you will receive. Keep seeking, and you
will find. Keep knocking, and the door will be opened to you. 10 For everyone
who asks, receives, and everyone who seeks, finds, and to everyone who
knocks, the door will be opened.
11 "You who are fathers, if your son asks for a fish, do you instead hand him a
snake? 12 Or if he asks for an egg, do you give him a scorpion? 13 So if you, sinful
as you are, know how to give good gifts to your children, how much more will
your heavenly Father give his Holy Spirit to those who ask him."

Isa Teaches About the Prince of the Demons

14 One day Isa cast out a demon from someone who couldn't speak. The
demon left, the person began to talk, and the crowds were amazed. 15 But
some of them said, "He simply uses Beelzebul, the prince of demons, to cast
out demons." 16 Others, only wanting to test Isa, demanded that he produce a
sign from Heaven.
17 But he knew what they all were thinking, so he told them, "A kingdom
divided within will collapse. A feuding home will fail. 18 You say I cast out
demons by Beelzebul. But if Shaitan is divided against himself that way, how
can his kingdom survive? 19 And if I cast out demons by Beelzebul, then by
whom do your own people cast them out? They themselves will condemn
what you say. 20 But if I cast out demons by the power of Allah, the kingdom
of Allah itself has come to you. 21 When a strong man, fully armed, guards
his own estate, his things are safe— 22 unless someone even stronger attacks
and overcomes the man's trusted defenses, defeats him, and distributes the
plunder.

23 "Anyone who isn't with me is against me, and whoever doesn't help me gather the crop, scatters it.

24 "When an evil spirit leaves a person, it ends up in the desert. Looking for a place to rest but finding none, it says, 'I'll just return to my former house.'
25 So it does, and discovers everything swept and in order. 26 Then it goes and
finds seven other spirits more evil than itself, and they all take up residence. And the result for that person is worse than ever."

27 As he was teaching these things, a woman in the crowd shouted out, "How blessed is the woman who bore you and nursed you!"

28 Isa replied, "In fact, blessed are all who hear the word of Allah and follow it."

Isa Teaches About the Sign of Yunus

29 As the crowds increased, Isa said, "This is an evil generation. It keeps asking
for a sign, but the only one I'll give is the sign of Yunus. 30 Just as Yunus was a
sign to the people of Nineveh, so the Son of Man will be to this generation.[a]

31 "On the Day of Judgment, the queen of the south[b] will stand up and condemn the people of this generation. For she traveled from a distant land to hear the wisdom of King Sulaiman, and something even greater than
Sulaiman is here. 32 And on the Day of Judgment, the people of Nineveh will
stand up and condemn this generation, for they repented at the preaching of Yunus,[c] and something even greater than Yunus is here.

Isa Teaches About the Light of True Understanding

33 "No one lights a lamp only to hide it or to stick it under a basket. It's put up on a stand to light the way for those inside.

34 "Your eye is like a lamp to provide you with light. When your eye is good, your whole being is bathed in light. But when it is bad, you are plunged into
darkness.[d] 35 Take care that the truth you possess is not actually darkness. 36 If
your way is well lit, with no dark places, then everything will be bright, like a brilliant lamp shining all around you."

Isa Criticizes the Religious Leaders

37 As Isa was speaking, a Pharisee invited him to dine with him. So he went
in and sat at the table. 38 The Pharisee noticed that, contrary to custom, Isa

---

a 11:30 Due to his refusal to proclaim the mercy of Allah to Israel's enemies, Prophet Yunus spent three days in the belly of a large fish, after which Allah miraculously freed him (see Yunus/Jonah 1–2). This was a picture foreshadowing how Isa would spend three days dead in a burial cave, after which he was resurrected (see Matthew 12:40).

b 11:31 *Queen of the south*—i.e., the Queen of Sheba. Sheba is in modern-day Yemen. Her meeting with King Sulaiman is described in 1 Kings 10:1-13.

c 11:32 See Yunus/Jonah 3:6-9.

d 11:34 In some contexts having a "good eye" means being generous (Proverbs 22:9) as opposed to the stinginess or enviousness of the "evil eye" (Proverbs 23:6; Matthew 20:15). The parallel context in Matthew 6:21-23 is talking about money and treasure so perhaps that is the meaning here also.

hadn't washed his hands before the meal. He, the host, was shocked. 39 Then
the Lord said to him, "You Pharisees clean what's on the outside—cups and
platters—but within you are full of greed and evil. 40 You foolish people! Didn't
the One who made the outside also make the inside? 41 So attend to the inside
by giving to the needy, and then you will be clean throughout.

42 "Woe to you, Pharisees! For you give a tenth of your mint, rue, and other
garden plants, but you ignore justice and love for Allah. The one should be
done without neglecting the other.

43 "Woe to you, Pharisees! For you bask in seats of honor in the prayer halls
and delight to be greeted in the markets. 44 Woe to you! For you are like hidden
graves walked on by the unwitting."[a]

45 A scholar of religious law replied, "Teacher, what you just said insults us
too!"

46 "Indeed," said Isa. "Woe also to you, scholars of religious law! For you
burden people with heavy demands, but you never lift so much as a finger to
lighten their loads. 47 Woe to you, for you erect memorials to the prophets, yet
it was your own ancestors who killed them. 48 So go right on endorsing the
activities of your ancestors—the killers of those whose memory you honor!
49 Allah in his wisdom said this about you: 'I will send them prophets and
emissaries. They will kill some, and persecute others.'

50 "This generation will be held responsible for the shed blood of all the
prophets since the world's foundation, 51 from the blood of Abel to the blood
of Zakariya, murdered between the altar and the temple.[b] Yes, I tell you, this
generation will be held responsible for it all.

52 "So woe to you, scholars of religious law! For you discard the key of
knowledge. You yourselves don't enter, and those attempting it, you obstruct."

53 As Isa was leaving, the scholars of religion and the Pharisees vigorously
opposed him. They peppered him with questions, 54 scheming to trap him in
something he might say.

Isa Warns Against Hypocrisy

12 Meanwhile, the crowd grew into the thousands, so large that people
were even stepping on each other. Isa addressed his disciples first,
saying, "Beware of the yeast of the Pharisees—their hypocrisy. 2 Everything
that's been covered up will be exposed, and everything hidden will be
discovered. 3 Whatever you might say in the dark will be heard in the light,
and what you speak in private will be proclaimed from the housetops.

---

a 11:44 The corruption of the Pharisees was of their hearts, and thus not outwardly visible (i.e., it was "unmarked"), but it defiled those who followed their ways as surely as touching a grave made a man ritually unclean.

b 11:51 The ancient Hebrews ordered the books of the Holy Scriptures differently than we do today. The death of Abel was the first murder (see Genesis 4:1-10), and, according to the old Hebrew order, the killing of Zakariya was the last one recorded (see 2 Chronicles 24:20-22).

[4] "Dear friends, don't be afraid of those who, after killing your body, can do nothing more. [5] Let me tell you who to fear—the One who, after killing the body, has the power to throw you into hell. To be sure, he's the One to fear!

[6] "Aren't five sparrows sold off for only two pennies?[c] But not one of them escapes Allah's notice. [7] He even counts every hair on your head. So don't be afraid. You are more valuable than many sparrows.

[8] "I tell you this, everyone who lays claim to me before man, the Son of Man will also lay claim to him before Allah's angels. [9] But anyone who rejects me before man will be rejected before Allah's angels. [10] And everyone who says something against the Son of Man will be forgiven, but anyone who denigrates Allah's Holy Spirit will not be forgiven.

[11] "So when you are brought to trial in prayer halls and before rulers and authorities, don't worry about how to defend yourself or what to say, [12] for at that time Allah's Holy Spirit will tell you what it is you should say."

A Parable About a Rich Fool

[13] Then someone from the crowd said, "Teacher, please tell my brother to share the family inheritance with me."

[14] Isa replied, "Hey, who appointed me to be a judge or probate officer over you?" [15] Then he said to all, "Look out for and avoid any greed you may have, because life isn't found in an abundance of possessions."

[16] Then he told them a parable. "A rich man owned a well producing farm.
[17] And he thought to himself, 'Hmm. What should I do? I don't have enough room to store all my crops. [18] I know! I'll tear down my barns and build bigger ones so I can store all my grain and other goods. [19] Then I'll sit back and say to myself, "Ah! You have enough stashed away to last for years. Relax! Eat, drink, and be merry!"'

[20] "But Allah said to him, 'You fool! Your life will be taken this very night, and everything you've saved will go to others.'

[21] "So it is for those who amass wealth but aren't rich with Allah."

Isa Teaches About Money and Possessions

[22] Then, turning to his disciples, Isa said, "That's why I tell you, don't consume yourselves with daily life—what you'll have to eat or wear. [23] There's more to life than food, and to your body than clothing. [24] Consider the ravens. They don't plant or harvest, and they don't have storerooms or barns. Yet Allah feeds them. You're worth far more than birds! [25] Can worry lengthen your life by even a moment? [26] If it can't do a little thing, why worry over bigger things?

[27] "Think about how lilies grow. They don't toil at labor or sew themselves clothes. But let me tell you, King Sulaiman himself in all his finery couldn't compete with them. [28] Given that Allah so beautifully adorns mere plants—here today but fuel tomorrow—he'll certainly provide for you, you doubters.

---

c 12:6 *Two pennies*—lit. "two assaria." An assarion was a coin worth 1/16 of a denarius, which in turn was a day's wage for a common laborer.

[29] "So don't chase around consumed by what to eat and drink. [30] That's what
the world's people seek. Your Father knows you need such things. [31] Instead,
pursue his kingdom, and he'll provide the rest.

[32] "Don't fear, little flock. Allah delights to give you the kingdom.

[33] "Sell your possessions and give to the needy. Make yourselves moneybags
that will never run out—an endless treasure in heaven which no thief can
steal or moth corrupt. [34] For wherever your treasure is, that's where your
heart will be.

Isa Teaches About His Return

[35] "Be dressed to go with your lamps lit, [36] like servants expecting their
master's return from a wedding. When he arrives and signals at the door, they
immediately let him in. [37] Those watching for his return will be rewarded. I
tell you, he'll dress himself for service, seat them at the table, and step up to
wait on them. [38] He might come in the middle of the night, or he might come
before dawn. But whenever he comes, those ready for him will be blessed.

[39] "Understand this: If a homeowner were to know exactly when a burglar
would show up, then he could easily prevent his house from being robbed.
[40] But since the Son of Man will come when you don't expect him, you should
be ready all the time."

[41] Then Peter asked, "Lord, does your illustration apply just to us or to
everyone?"

[42] The Lord responded, "Where can a master find a faithful and wise servant
to manage rations for his household staff? [43] A servant like that—one whom
the master upon his return discovers caring for responsibilities—will be
highly rewarded. [44] Indeed, the master will appoint such a one to oversee
the entire estate. [45] But what if that servant thinks, 'My master won't return
for a long time.' And he takes to beating those below him, male and female,
and to feasting and drunkenness. [46] Well, when the master returns it will be
a complete shock to him. And the master will thrash him severely and expel
him to join the unfaithful.

[47] "So a servant who knows what the master wants but isn't concerned
enough to do it will be severely punished. [48] But someone who doesn't know,
yet does things worthy of a beating, will be only lightly punished. To all those
assigned much, from them much will be required, and to all those entrusted
with much, from them, much will be expected.

Isa Will Be the Source of Division

[49] "I've come to start a fire on earth, and I wish it were already lit. [50] But I
am going to be plunged into suffering, and I'm so burdened until it's over!
[51] Do you think I've come to bring peace to the earth? Not at all. I've come to
bring division. [52] From now on, homes will be divided. A family of five will
split three against two and two against three.

[53] 'Father will be divided against son,
and son against father.
Mother against daughter,
and daughter against mother.
And mother-in-law against daughter-in-law,
And daughter-in-law against mother-in-law.'"[a]

Isa Teaches About the Signs of the Times

[54] Then Isa said to the crowds, "When you see clouds forming in the west, you
say, 'It's going to rain.' And it does. [55] And when a south wind blows, you say,
'Today will be hot.' And so it is. [56] You hypocrites. You predict the weather by
analyzing earth and sky, but you can't do the same with this present time.
[57] Why don't you judge for yourselves what's right?

[58] "If your accuser is bringing you to the authorities, do all you can along
the way to settle the matter. Otherwise, he'll drag you before the judge, and
the judge will hand you over to the officer, and the officer will throw you into
prison. [59] And let me tell you, if that happens, you won't get out until you've
paid the very last penny."[b]

Isa Calls People to Repentance

13 Then, people informed Isa that Pilate had murdered some Galileans as
they offered sacrifices in the temple. [2] Isa asked them, "Do you imagine
those Galileans were somehow more sinful than others from Galilee? Is that
why they experienced such a death? [3] Not at all. Listen to me. If you don't
repent, you'll all perish too. [4] There's also the eighteen killed by the Siloam
tower's collapse. Do you suppose that means they were al-Quds's worst
culprits? [5] Not at all. Listen to me. If you don't repent, you'll all perish too."

A Parable About a Barren Fig Tree

[6] Then Isa told this parable: "A man planted a fig tree in his garden. He would
check it for fruit, but there was none. [7] So he said to his gardener, 'I've come
for three years expecting fruit from this tree, but there's nothing. Cut it down.
Why let it deplete the soil?'

[8] "But the gardener said, 'Sir, let it be for another year. I'll dig around it and
add manure. [9] Then, if it yields fruit next year, great. If not, we'll cut it down.'"

Isa Heals on the Day of Rest

[10] One Day of Rest, Isa was teaching in a prayer hall. [11] A woman was there who,
for eighteen years, had been bent over by an evil spirit and so was unable to
stand straight. [12] When Isa saw her, he called to her, saying, "Dear woman,
you are released from your affliction." [13] Then he put his hands on her, and
immediately she stood straight and began praising Allah.

---

a 12:53 See Micah 7:6.

b 12:59 *Penny*—lit. "lepta." A lepta was the smallest Greek coin, worth about 1/128 of a denarius.

14 But the prayer hall leader was angry that Isa had healed on a Day of Rest. And he said to all attending, "There are six days of the week for work. Come on those days for healing, not on the Day of Rest!"

15 But the Lord replied, "You hypocrites. Don't each of you work on the Day of Rest when you untie your ox or your donkey in the stall and lead it out to drink? 16 This woman is a daughter of Ibrahim. Shaitan has held her captive for eighteen years. Shouldn't she be untied from her bonds on the Day of Rest?"

17 That response humiliated all his enemies, but the crowd rejoiced at all the wonderful things he did.

A Parable About a Mustard Seed

18 Then Isa said, "Do you know what the kingdom of Allah is like, and how to describe it? 19 It's like a tiny mustard seed. A man plants it in his garden, it grows up, and it becomes like a tree with birds making nests in its branches."

A Parable About Yeast

20 Then he asked, "What else is the kingdom of Allah like? 21 It's like yeast. A woman puts some in her bread dough, and though she makes a huge batch,[a] the yeast works its way through the whole thing."

Isa Teaches About the Way to Allah

22 Isa went through various towns and villages, teaching as he made his way to al-Quds. 23 And a person asked him, "Lord, will only a few people be saved?"

He replied, 24 "Do your utmost to enter through the narrow door. I assure you, many who try to enter will fail. 25 Then, when the master of the house gets up and locks the door, you'll start knocking from outside, pleading, 'Lord, open up for us!' But he'll say, 'I don't know you or where you're from.' 26 You'll respond, 'But we ate and drank with you, and you taught in our town!' 27 And he'll reply, 'Listen to me, I don't know you or where you're from. Get away from me, all you experts in evil!'[b] 28 Then you will weep and gnash your teeth, seeing Ibrahim, Ishaq, Yaqub, and all the prophets in the kingdom of Allah, but you thrown out. 29 And people will arrive from all over, from east and west, north and south, to dine in the kingdom of Allah. 30 And so it will be: those at the back will come to the front, and those at the front will go to the back."

Isa Grieves Over al-Quds

31 At that time some Pharisees approached, telling Isa, "You should get out of here. Herod[c] wants to kill you!"

32 But he said to them, "Go tell this to that vicious fox: 'Today and tomorrow I'll continue to cast out demons and heal. And on the third day I'll reach my goal.'

---

a 13:21 *Huge batch*—lit. "three sata." This is about 20 kg (44 lb) of flour.

b 13:27 See Zabur/Psalm 6:8.

c 13:31 This is Herod Antipas (see footnote on 3:1).

33 “So regardless, today, tomorrow, and the next day I must proceed on. For it’s unthinkable that a prophet could perish outside al-Quds!

34 “Oh, al-Quds, al-Quds, you who kill the prophets and stone Allah’s messengers! I’ve so often wanted to gather your children together, like a hen with her chicks beneath her wings. But you have refused. 35 So now, your house is empty.[d] You will not see me again, I tell you, until you say, ‘Blessed is the one who comes in the name of the Lord!’”[e]

Isa Heals on the Day of Rest

14 One day, Isa attended a dinner at a Pharisee leader’s home. It was during a Day of Rest, and others attending watched Isa closely. 2 Right by him was a man with badly swollen limbs. 3 So, Isa posed a question for the experts in religion and the Pharisees: “Does the law allow healing on a Day of Rest, or not?” 4 They didn’t respond. Isa then touched the man, healed him, and sent him away. 5 Then he said to them, “If you have a son or cow which, on a Day of Rest, falls into a deep pit, don’t you immediately pull them out?” 6 And they couldn’t give a suitable reply.

Isa Teaches About Humility

7 Isa noticed how the dinner guests were taking the seats of honor. So he told them this: 8 “When you’re invited to a wedding feast, don’t sit in the seat of honor. Someone more distinguished than you may also have been invited, 9 and the one who invited you both will have to approach you, saying, ‘Give your seat to this person.’ Then in disgrace you’ll have to take a seat at the end of the table.

10 “Instead, when invited sit in the least honorable place. Then your host may step up and say to you, ‘Friend, please move up here.’ Then you will be honored in front of all the other guests. 11 For those who promote themselves will be humbled, and those who humble themselves will be promoted.”

12 Then he also spoke to his host. “When you put on a luncheon or a banquet, don’t invite your friends, siblings, relatives, or rich neighbors. For your only reward will be a return invitation. 13 Instead, when you give a banquet, invite people who are poor, disabled, lame, and blind. 14 Then you will be blessed. Because they will not be able to repay you, you will be rewarded at the resurrection of the righteous.”

A Parable About a Great Feast

15 Hearing all that, someone sitting with Isa exclaimed, “How blessed are those who banquet in the kingdom of Allah!”

16 Isa replied with this: “A man was preparing a great feast to which he had invited many guests. 17 When the banquet was ready, he sent his servant to notify them. ‘Come!,’ he said. ‘The banquet is ready!’ 18 But they all begged off with excuses. One said to the servant, ‘I just bought a field and need to see it.

d 13:35 See Jeremiah 22:5.
e 13:35 Zabur/Psalm 118:26.

Please excuse me.' 19 Another said, 'I just bought five pairs of oxen and I'm on
my way to try them out. Please excuse me.' 20 Another said, 'I got married and
can't come.'

21 "The servant returned and told all this to his master. Angry, the owner
of the house told his servant, 'Go quickly into the streets and alleys of the
town and invite the poor, disabled, blind, and lame.' 22 The servant obeyed
and reported back, 'Sir, what you said has been done, and there's still room.'
23 So his master said, 'Go out to the roads and lanes and urge people to come,
so that the house will be full. 24 Let me tell you, absolutely none of those I first
invited will taste a bite of my banquet!'"

Isa Teaches About the Cost of Being His Disciple

25 Large crowds were following Isa. Turning to face them, he said, 26 "Whoever
comes to me without hating their father, mother, wife, children, brothers,
sisters, and even their own life, cannot be my disciple.[a] 27 And whoever does
not carry their own cross and follow me, cannot be my disciple.[b]

28 "If you wanted to build a great tower, wouldn't you first sit down and
count the cost to see if you have enough funds to complete it? 29 Otherwise, you
may just finish its foundation, run out of money, and become a laughingstock
to those watching. 30 They'll say, 'Ha! There's the one who started the great
tower, but he couldn't finish it!'

31 "Or, suppose a king opposes his rival in war. Doesn't he first sit in counsel
to determine if his 10,000 soldiers can handle the 20,000 marching against
him? 32 If not, while still far off he'll send ahead a delegation to plead for
peace. 33 So likewise, consider—unless you give up everything you have, you
cannot be my disciple.

34 "Salt is a good thing. But if it somehow becomes tasteless, how can you
ever restore it? 35 It's no good for the soil or even added to a manure pile. It's
just thrown away. Whoever has ears should use them to listen!"

A Parable About a Lost Sheep

15 Many tax collectors and moral outcasts were coming to hear Isa teach.
2 So the Pharisees and scholars of religion complained, "This fellow
receives flagrant sinners. He even eats with them!"

3 So Isa told them this parable. 4 "Suppose someone you know has a hundred
sheep and one of them gets lost. What will he do? Won't he leave the ninety-
nine in the field and search for the lost one until he finds it? 5 And when he
finds it, he puts it on his shoulders, rejoicing. 6 Upon arriving home, he calls

---

a 14:26 Isa does not literally want us to hate our family members, but to put our allegiance to Allah far above our loyalty to family, so that if it comes to choosing between them, we will choose to follow Allah. In such cases he has promised to provide us with new spiritual family members (see Mark 10:30).

b 14:27 Following Isa requires much more that fulfilling religious duties—it involves crucifying our own agenda in order to live for Allah's priorities, trusting that his agenda is the only one that ultimately matters, and that he will provide what we really need along the way.

together his friends and neighbors, saying, ‘Rejoice with me! I’ve found my lost sheep!’ 7 I’m telling you, there’s likewise more joy in heaven over one repentant sinner than over ninety-nine righteous people who don’t need to repent!

A Parable About a Lost Coin

8 “Suppose a woman has ten silver coins[c] and loses one. Won’t she light a lamp, sweep her house, and search carefully until she finds it? 9 And when she finds it, she invites her friends and neighbors over, saying, ‘Rejoice with me! I’ve found my lost coin!’ 10 I’m telling you, there is likewise joy among Allah’s angels when even one sinner repents.”

A Parable About a Wayward Son

11 Isa continued. “A man had two sons. 12 The younger one told his father, ‘Give me my share of the estate.’ So the man divided his wealth between his sons.

13 “A few days later the younger one packed up, moved to a far-off land, and proceeded to squander his fortune on wild living. 14 When he had spent it all, a severe famine hit the area, and he began to starve. 15 So he went and hired himself out to a local citizen, who put the young man in his fields to feed pigs. 16 And he got so hungry, he could have filled up even on the bean pods eaten by the pigs. No one gave him a thing to eat.

17 “When he finally came to his senses, he said to himself, ‘All my father’s hired servants have more than enough food, but here I am, dying of hunger! 18 I’m leaving. I’ll return to my father and say to him, “Father, I’ve sinned against Heaven[d] and against you. 19 I’m no longer worthy to be your son. Please, just hire me as one of your servants.”’

20 “So he got up and went back to his father. But while he was still a way off, his father saw him approaching. Filled with deep love, he ran to his son, held him tightly, and kissed him. 21 The son said to him, ‘Father, I’ve sinned against heaven and against you. I’m no longer worthy to be your son.’

22 “But the father said to his servants, ‘Quick! Bring the best robe and place it on him. Put a ring on his hand[e] and sandals on his feet. 23 And get the fattened calf and butcher it. Let’s eat and celebrate! 24 For this son of mine was dead but has come back to life! He was lost, but now he’s found!’ So they began to celebrate.

25 “Meanwhile, the man’s older son was in the fields. When he approached the house, he heard music and dancing. 26 So he called to one of the servants and asked what was going on. 27 The reply came: ‘Your brother is back! And to celebrate his safe return, your father has killed the fattened calf.’

28 “But the older brother became angry and wouldn’t go in. So his father came out and pleaded with him. 29 But he said to his father, ‘All these years I’ve

---

c 15:8 *Silver coins*—lit. “ten drachmas.” A drachma was a silver coin, worth about a day’s wages for a common laborer.

d 15:18 The Hebrews, in order to avoid using the name of the Most High in a frivolous manner (see Exodus 20:7), often used the word “Heaven” instead (see also 20:4).

e 15:22 This was a symbolic reaffirmation of his rights as a son.

served you and not once have I disobeyed. But you've never given me even a young goat for a feast with my friends. 30 Yet after this son of yours devours your wealth with prostitutes, for him you butcher the fattened calf!'

31 "His father said to him, 'Son, you've always stayed with me, and all I have is yours. 32 But we had to celebrate and rejoice. Your brother, once dead, has come back to life! He was lost, but now he's found!'"

A Parable About a Clever Manager

16 Isa also said this to his disciples. "There was a rich man whose household manager was accused of squandering the estate. 2 So the employer summoned him and said, 'What's this I hear about you? Prepare an accounting of your activities, for you will no longer be manager.'

3 "The manager said to himself, 'What should I do? My boss is firing me! I'm not strong enough for manual labor, and I'm ashamed to beg. 4 Ah, I know what to do! Then, when I lose my job, I'll be welcome elsewhere!'

5 "So he called in everyone indebted to his employer. He asked the first, 'How much do you owe him?' 6 The man replied, '100 large containers of olive oil.'[a] So the manager told him, 'Here's your bill. Quick. Sit down and write that it's only 50.'

7 "Then he said to another, 'And how much do you owe?' The man replied, '100 large bins of wheat.'[b] 'Here's your bill,' the manager said. 'Make it only 80.'

8 "As for the employer, he commended the corrupt manager for being so clever. And so it is—the cleverness of the world's own as they relate to their peers surpasses that of the children of light. 9 I'm telling you, therefore, use your mere worldly wealth to make friends for yourselves. Then, when it's gone, they'll welcome you into an eternal home.

10 "Whoever is faithful in small matters will be faithful in big ones. Likewise, whoever is dishonest in small matters will be dishonest in big ones. 11 Therefore, if you are not faithful with mere worldly wealth, who will entrust you with the real thing? 12 And if you are not faithful with what belongs to another, who will give you something for yourself?

13 "No servant can attend to two masters. You will hate one and love the other; you will be devoted to one and despise the other. You cannot serve both Allah and money."

14 Hearing all this, the Pharisees scoffed at him, for they loved money. 15 But Isa said to them, "In front of people you parade around as righteous. But Allah knows your hearts. What's applauded among people is repulsive to Allah.

---

a 16:6 The unit used in the original is "baths." One bath was about nine gallons (33 liters) of olive oil. It would take a typical laborer over three years to earn enough to buy 100 baths of olive oil.

b 16:7 The unit in the original is the "cor," equal to about 11 bushels (390 liters). It would take a typical laborer roughly ten years to earn enough to buy 100 cors of wheat.

Isa Teaches About Allah's Law

16 "Until Yahya arrived, the law and the Prophets stood alone. Since then, the
good news about Allah's kingdom is announced, and people are eager to
enter it.[c] 17 But heaven and earth are more likely to vanish than a tiny bit of
the law to drop out.
18 "Any man who divorces his wife and marries another commits adultery.
And a man who marries a woman divorced from her husband commits
adultery."

A Parable About a Rich Man and a Poor Man

19 Isa said, "There was a rich man who dressed in fine clothes and lived in
constant luxury. 20 At his gate was laid a poor man named Lazarus, covered
with sores. 21 He longed for scraps from the rich man's table, and dogs would
lick his sores.
22 "In time, the poor man died, and angels carried him away to be with
Ibrahim. The rich man also died and was buried. 23 Tormented in hell, he
looked up and saw Ibrahim far off with Lazarus at his side.
24 "The rich man shouted, 'Father Ibrahim! Have mercy on me! Send Lazarus
to dip his finger in some water and cool my tongue. I'm in anguish in these
flames!'
25 "But Ibrahim replied, 'Son, remember that you enjoyed good things in
life while Lazarus suffered. Now he is here being comforted, but you are in
anguish. 26 Furthermore, a great chasm lies fixed between us. No one wishing
to pass from here to you can do so. Likewise from there to us, no one can
cross.'
27 "The rich man responded, 'Then please, Father Ibrahim, send him to my
father's home! 28 I have five brothers. Lazarus can warn them not to end up in
this place of torment!'
29 "But Ibrahim said, 'They have the writings of Musa and the prophets. Your
brothers should listen to them.'
30 "The rich man replied, 'No, Father Ibrahim! If a person who's died goes to
them, they'll repent!'
31 "But Ibrahim said, 'If they won't listen to Musa and the prophets, they
won't be convinced even by someone who returns from the dead.'"

Isa Teaches About Forgiveness and Faith

17 Isa said to his disciples, "Enticements to sin are inevitable, but woe to
anyone who offers them! 2 Better to be thrown into the sea wearing
a millstone necklace than to entice one of these little ones to sin. 3 Watch
yourselves!
"If your brother or sister sins, rebuke them. And if they repent, forgive
them. 4 Even if they sin against you seven times a day and each time return
saying, 'I'm sorry,' forgive them."

---

c 16:16 Or "... people are urged to enter it."

[5] The emissaries replied to the Lord, "Expand our faith!"

[6] But the Lord responded, "If you have faith, though it's as small as a mustard seed, you can say to this mulberry tree, 'Uproot and replant yourself in the sea,' and it will obey you.

[7] "When a servant returns from plowing or caring for sheep, what master says to him, 'Come, sit down and eat'? [8] Instead he says, 'Prepare my meal, dress for service, and wait on me while I eat and drink. After that you can eat and drink.' [9] Or does a master thank a servant for following orders? [10] Likewise, when you've done everything Allah commands, you should say, 'We're mere servants. We've simply done our duty.'"

Isa Heals Ten Leprous Men

[11] Proceeding on to al-Quds, Isa passed through the area between Galilee and Samaria. [12] As he entered a certain village, ten lepers stood at a distance [13] shouting, "Isa, Master, have mercy on us!"

[14] He looked at them and said, "Go show yourselves to the priests." And as they went, they were healed.

[15] Seeing himself well, one of them came back to Isa shouting praises to Allah. [16] Then he threw himself down face first at Isa's feet and thanked him. Now, the man was a Samaritan.[a]

[17] So Isa asked, "Weren't ten men healed? Where are the other nine? [18] Has no one returned to glorify Allah except this foreigner?" [19] Then Isa said to the man, "Stand up and go. Your faith has healed you."

Isa Teaches About the Coming of the Kingdom

[20] Some Pharisees asked Isa, "When will the kingdom of Allah come?"

He replied, "The kingdom of Allah is not going to appear as something visible. [21] People won't say, 'Here it is!' or 'It's located there.' The kingdom of Allah is already among you!"

[22] Then he said to his disciples, "The time is coming when you will long to see one of the days of the Son of Man, but won't. [23] People will say, 'He's here!,' or 'He's there!' But don't go out and look. [24] For the Son of Man on his day will be like lightning which flashes and lights up the sky from one end to the other. [25] But first he must suffer many things and be rejected by this generation.

[26] "As things were in Nuh's day, so they will be at the time of the Son of Man. [27] People carried on eating, drinking, and marrying right up to the day Nuh entered the ark. And then the flood came and destroyed them all.

[28] "And in Lut's day as well, people carried on eating and drinking, buying and selling, farming and building, [29] until the time Lut left Sodom, and then burning sulfur rained down from heaven and destroyed them all. [30] And so things will be until the day the Son of Man is revealed. [31] In that time a person on top of their house should not go in for their possessions, and a person out in the field should not return home. [32] Remember what happened to Lut's

---

a 17:16 See footnote on 10:33.

wife![b] 33 Whoever seeks to save their life will lose it, but whoever gives up their life will save it. 34 I tell you, during that night two people will be lying in one bed; one will be taken up, the other left behind.[c] 35-36 Two women will be grinding flour together; one will be taken, the other left behind."[d]

37 Isa's disciples asked, "Lord, where will this happen?"

He replied, "Wherever corpses lie, there the vultures gather."[e]

A Parable About a Persistent Widow

18 Isa told his disciples a parable to show that they should always pray and not lose heart. 2 "In a certain city there was a judge who didn't fear Allah or respect people. 3 A local widow kept going to him, saying, 'Give me justice against my opponent.' 4 Refusing for a while, he finally said to himself, 'I don't fear Allah or respect people. 5 But this widow is becoming a problem. I'll see she gets justice. Otherwise, her incessant appeals will wear me out!'"

6 Then the Lord said, "Consider what the unjust judge said. 7 Won't Allah himself grant justice to his chosen people crying out to him day and night? Will he keep putting them off? 8 I tell you, he'll grant them justice promptly. However, when the Son of Man returns, will he find anyone on earth with real faith?"

A Parable About a Pharisee and a Tax Collector

9 Then Isa directed this parable to those who trusted in themselves—that they were righteous but others worthy of disdain. 10 "Two men went up to the temple to pray, a Pharisee and a tax collector. 11 The Pharisee stood by himself and prayed this: 'I thank you, Allah, that I am not like other people—greedy, dishonest, adulterous ... and certainly not like that tax collector! 12 I fast twice a week. I give away a tenth of my income.'

13 "But the tax collector stood at a distance, reluctant to even look up toward heaven. Instead, he struck himself on the chest, saying, 'Oh Allah, be merciful to me, a sinner!' 14 I tell you, the tax collector went home right with Allah, but not the Pharisee. For those who promote themselves will be humbled, and those who humble themselves will be promoted."

---

b 17:32 Although she was led out of Sodom, in her heart Lut's wife wanted to stay there. This desire lead to her death (see Genesis 19:23-26).

c 17:34 *Taken up ... left behind*—There are two main interpretations of these words: 1) The Lord Isa will take his own followers, and others will be left for punishment. 2) Sinners will be taken for judgment, and his followers will be left. In any case it is obvious that there will be a division, and the criteria will be a person's faith and life.

d 17:35-36 Some manuscripts include verse 36: "And there will be two people in the field, and one will be taken, and the other left behind."

e 17:37 There are many interpretations of this verse. Here are two of the most probable: 1) Where moral disintegration reaches its apogee, Allah's judgment will be unavoidable. 2) The return of the Messiah will be obvious to everyone just like a gathering of vultures clearly indicates that there is a carcass nearby.

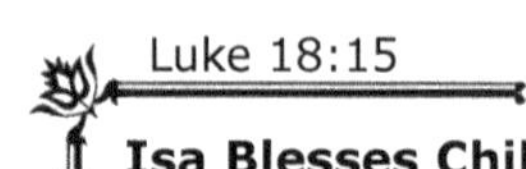

Isa Blesses Children

[15] People even brought little children to Isa so he would touch them. When the disciples saw that, they rebuked them.

[16] But Isa called the children to himself and said, "Let the children come to me. Don't stop them. For the kingdom of Allah belongs to people like these.
[17] I tell you the truth, whoever doesn't receive the kingdom of Allah like a child will never enter it."

Isa Talks With a Rich Man

[18] A man of high rank asked Isa a question: "Good Teacher, what must I do to inherit eternal life?"

[19] "Why do you call me good?" Isa replied. "No one but Allah alone is truly good. [20] You know the commandments: 'Do not commit adultery. Do not murder. Do not steal. Do not testify falsely. Honor your father and mother.'"[a]

[21] The man replied, "I've kept all those since the time I was young."

[22] Hearing that, Isa said to him, "There's still something you haven't done. Sell everything you own and distribute the money among the poor. You'll have treasure in heaven! And then, come, follow me."

[23] Hearing that, the man became dejected, for he was extremely rich.

[24] When Isa saw his reaction, he said, "Prosperous people find it very hard
to enter the kingdom of Allah. [25] It's easier for a camel to pass through the eye of a needle than for a rich person to enter the kingdom of Allah."

[26] Those who heard that said, "Then who can be saved?"

[27] He replied, "What's impossible for people is possible for Allah."

[28] Then Peter responded, "Well, we left what was ours and followed you."

[29] To that Isa replied, "I assure you that anyone who, for the sake of Allah's kingdom, has given up their home, spouse, siblings, parents, or children,
[30] will receive many times as much in this life, and in the world to come—eternal life."

Isa Again Predicts His Death

[31] Isa took the twelve emissaries aside and said, "Listen, we're going up to al-Quds, and all the prophecies written by the prophets about the Son of Man
will come true. [32] He will be handed over to the pagans, mocked, insulted,
and spit upon. [33] They will flog him and kill him. But on the third day he will return to life."

[34] But the emissaries didn't grasp any of this. The entire concept was obscure to them, so they failed to understand what he was saying.

Isa Heals a Blind Beggar

[35] As Isa approached Jericho, a blind man was sitting beside the road, begging.
[36] When he heard the crowd moving along, he asked what was happening.

---

a 18:20 See Exodus 20:12-16; Deuteronomy 5:16-20.

[37] They told him that Isa of Nazareth was passing by. [38] So he started to shout,
"Isa, Son of Dawud,[b] have mercy on me!"

[39] The people in front angrily told him to keep quiet.

But he yelled even louder, "Son of Dawud, have mercy on me!"

[40] Then Isa stopped and said that the man should be brought to him. When
he was near, Isa asked him, [41] "What do you want me to do for you?"

The man replied, "Lord, let me see again."

[42] And Isa said to him, "Receive back your sight. Your faith has healed you."
[43] The man's sight was instantly restored, and he followed Isa, glorifying Allah.
And all the people, seeing what happened, praised Allah.

Isa Speaks With a Tax Collector

19 Then Isa entered Jericho and was passing through the town. [2] One of
the residents, a man named Zacchaeus, was a chief tax collector. And he
was rich. [3] Zacchaeus tried to get a look at Isa, but the crowd blocked his view,
for he was quite short. [4] So, in order to see Isa when he walked by, Zacchaeus
ran ahead and climbed a fig tree along the way.

[5] When Isa reached that spot, he looked up at Zacchaeus and said to him,
"Zacchaeus, quick, come down. I need to stay in your home today."

[6] Zacchaeus quickly got down and gladly received Isa. [7] But the people all
around grumbled, saying. "He's gone to stay with a disgusting sinner!"

[8] But Zacchaeus stood before Isa and announced, "Lord, I am giving half my property to the poor. And whoever I cheated on their taxes, I'll repay four times as much!"

[9] Isa responded, "Today, salvation has come to this home, for even this man
is a son of Ibrahim.[c] [10] For the Son of Man came to seek and to save people
who are lost."

A Parable About Ten Servants

[11] When the people had heard that, and because he was near to al-Quds, Isa
continued with a parable—for they thought the kingdom of Allah was about
to dawn. [12] He said, "A nobleman was set to travel to a distant land. There he'd
be crowned and then return home as king. [13] So he gathered together ten of
his servants and divided among them a large amount of silver,[d] saying, 'Invest
this for me while I'm away.' [14] But his people hated him, and they followed his
departure with a delegation saying: 'We don't want that man to rule over us!'

---

b 18:38 *Son of Dawud*—one of the titles of the Messiah. According to the prophets, the expected Messiah (i.e., the righteous king and redeemer) would be a descendant of King Dawud (see Isaiah 11:1-5; Jeremiah 23:5-6).

c 19:9 Prophet Ibrahim, having been declared righteous by Allah because of his faith (see Genesis 15:6), has become known as the father of all believers (see Romans 4:11-12). Although Zacchaeus was a physical descendant of Ibrahim, here he showed himself to be a son of Ibrahim in a spiritual sense (see John 8:39; Galatians 3:29).

d 19:13 Lit. "He gave them ten minas." In other words, each received one mina. A mina was an ancient Greek coin that was worth one hundred days' wages of a common laborer.

15 "After the man had been crowned, he returned and summoned the
servants to whom he had given the silver. He wanted a report about their
investments. 16 The first servant arrived and reported, 'Master, the tenth of
your silver has grown ten times over.'

17 "The king said, 'Excellent! You're a fine servant. Because you've been
faithful with a little, you're to rule over ten cities!'

18 "Then the second servant came and reported, 'Master, with your silver I
have made five times the original.'

19 "And the king said to that one, 'You're to rule over five cities!'

20 "But another servant came and reported, 'Master, here's your silver. I've
kept it hidden away in a cloth. 21 I was afraid of you. You're a hard man. You
take what you didn't invest and harvest what you didn't plant.'

22 "The king said to him, 'Your own mouth condemns you, you worthless
servant. If you knew that I'm a hard man, taking what I didn't invest and
harvesting what I didn't plant, 23 why didn't you deposit my money in a bank?
Then, when I returned, I could have received it back with interest.'

24 "Then the king ordered his attendants, 'Take the silver from him and give
it to the one who has ten portions.'

25 "'But, master,' they said, 'he already has ten!'

26 "The king replied, 'Indeed! All those who have produced will be given
more. But whoever has not, even what they possess will be taken away. 27 And
as for those enemies of mine who didn't want me to be their king, bring them
here, and in my presence execute them.'"

Isa Approaches al-Quds in Triumph

28 After telling that parable, Isa continued his journey, walking ahead of his
disciples toward al-Quds. 29 When he approached Bethphage and Bethany,
located on what is called the Mount of Olives, he told two disciples to go on
ahead, 30 "Enter that village over there. As you do, you'll see a donkey colt
leashed up which no one has ever ridden. Untie it and bring it here. 31 And if
anyone asks, 'Why are you untying it?' just say, 'The Lord needs it.'"

32 So the two went and found it, just as Isa had said. 33 As they were untying
it, the owners asked them, "Why are you untying the colt?"

34 The two replied, "The Lord needs it." 35 So they led the colt to Isa and put
their cloaks on it for him to sit on.[a]

36 As he rode along toward al-Quds, people spread their cloaks before him
on the road. 37 When he approached the spot where the road starts down the
Mount of Olives, all his many disciples began to cheer, praising Allah for all
the miracles they'd seen:

> 38 "Blessed is the king who comes in the name of the Lord![b]
> Peace in heaven! Glory to the heights!"

---

a 19:35 Isa entered al-Quds as a peaceful and humble king riding on a donkey and not armed with a sword and riding on a war-horse, as would have been expected for a king of his time.

b 19:38 Zabur/Psalm 118:26.

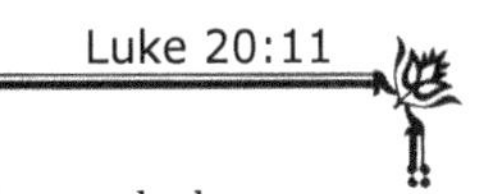

[39] But some of the Pharisees in the crowd said, "Teacher, rebuke your
disciples!"
[40] He replied, "If they keep quiet, I tell you the stones will shout!"

Isa Weeps Over al-Quds

[41] As Isa drew near and saw the city, he wept over it, [42] saying, "If you, especially
you, had only known on this day what could bring you peace! But now it's
hidden from you. [43] The time is coming upon you when your enemies will
build ramparts against you, surround you, and lay siege to you all around.
[44] They will crush you and your children within, and won't leave a single stone
standing—all because you did not recognize when your salvation arrived."[c]

Isa Cleanses the Temple

[45] Then Isa entered the temple and drove out the merchants, [46] telling them,
"It's written in the Scriptures, 'My house will be a house of prayer.'[d] But you've
made it 'a den of thieves.'"[e]
[47] After that, he taught daily in the temple. The head priests, the scholars
of religion, and other community leaders sought how to kill him. [48] But they
couldn't decide what to do, for all the people listening to him were captivated.

People Challenge Isa's Authority

20 One day, as Isa was teaching the people and proclaiming the good
news in the temple, the head priests, the scholars of religion and the
elders approached him [2] and said, "Explain. What authorizes you to do all
these things? Who gave you the right?"
[3] But Isa said to them, "Well then, I also have a question for you. Tell me,
[4] did Heaven authorize Yahya to perform ritual washings, or was it just a
human affair?"
[5] They discussed the question among themselves: "If we say 'Heaven,' he'll
ask why we didn't believe Yahya. [6] But if we say 'Human,' the people will stone
us, for they believe Yahya was a prophet!" [7] So they replied that they didn't
know.
[8] Then Isa responded in turn, "Then I won't tell you what authorizes me to
do these things."

A Parable About Evil Tenants

[9] Then Isa told the people this parable: "A man planted a vineyard,[f] leased it
to some farmers, and moved far away for a long period. [10] At harvest time he
sent a servant to the tenants to collect his share of the crop. But the farmers
beat up the servant and put him out empty-handed. [11] So the owner sent

---

c 19:44 This prophesy was fulfilled when the Romans completely destroyed al-Quds in A.D. 70.

d 19:46 Isaiah 56:7.

e 19:46 See Jeremiah 7:11.

f 20:9 Compare Isaiah 5:1-7.

another servant, but the tenants also beat him up, insulted him, and put him
out empty-handed. [12] He sent yet a third servant, but they severely injured
him and threw him out.

[13] "So the owner of the vineyard asked himself, 'What should I do? I'll send my dear son. They'll surely respect him.'

[14] "But when the farmers saw his son, they schemed together, 'He's the heir.
Let's kill him. Then the estate will be ours!' [15] So they dragged him out of the
vineyard and killed him.

"Now, what will the owner of the vineyard do to those farmers? [16] He'll go
and destroy them and lease the vineyard to others."

Those listening to Isa responded, "Surely not!"

[17] Isa looked at them and said, "Then what does this Scripture mean?

> 'The stone the builders rejected
> has become the cornerstone.'[a]

[18] Everyone who stumbles over that stone will be smashed, and anyone it falls upon will be crushed."

[19] The scholars of religion and the head priests wanted to arrest Isa immediately, for they knew he had directed the parable against them. But they feared the people.

Isa Teaches About Taxes

[20] Watching Isa closely, they sent spies pretending to be sincere. They wanted
Isa to incriminate himself. Then he could be turned in and subjected to the
Roman governor's jurisdiction. [21] So they asked him, "Teacher, we know you
speak and instruct what is right. You show no partiality, and teach only the
truth about the way of Allah. [22] So, is it lawful for us to pay taxes to Caesar or
not?"

[23] Seeing through their ploy, Isa said to them, [24] "Show me a Roman coin.[b]
Whose picture and name are on it?"

"Caesar's," they replied.

[25] So he said to them, "Then give to Caesar what is Caesar's, and to Allah what is Allah's."

[26] So they failed to trap him in his response before the people. And marveling at his answer, they fell silent.

Isa Teaches About the Resurrection

[27] Then Isa was approached by some Sadducees[c] —religious leaders who
claim that the dead do not return to life. [28] They asked him this: "Teacher,

---

a 20:17 Zabur/Psalm 118:22.

b 20:24 *Roman coin*—lit. "a denarius."

c 20:27 *Sadducees*—an aristocratic religious party of the Hebrews whose members rejected the idea of the resurrection of the dead and did not believe in angels or spirits. The Sadducees had major influence in the high council.

Musa wrote in our Scriptures that if a married man dies without a child, then
his brother should marry the woman and produce an offspring in honor of
his dead brother.[d] 29 Now, there were once seven brothers. The oldest married
but died childless. 30 Likewise the second. 31 In turn the third brother married
the widow, and so on through to the seventh. But all died without having a
child. 32 After that, the woman also died. 33 So, at the time when people return
to life, whose wife will she be, for all seven were married to her?"
34 Isa replied to them, "In this age, people marry and are given in marriage.
35 But in the age to come, those worthy of it—worthy of returning to life after
death—will neither marry nor be given in marriage. 36 Like angels, they'll
never die, being children of Allah and the resurrection.
37 "But whether the dead are brought back to life, Musa himself revealed
this in the passage about the burning bush. There he called the Lord 'the God
of Ibrahim, the God of Ishaq, and the God of Yaqub.'[e] 38 He's not God of the
dead but of the living, for they are all alive through him."
39 Some of the scholars of religion responded, "Well said, Teacher!" 40 And
none of them dared to question him again.

Isa Teaches About the Messiah

41 Then Isa posed a question for them. "How can people claim that the Messiah
descends from Dawud? 42 For Dawud himself wrote in the book of the Zabur:

> 'The Lord said to my Lord,
> Sit at my right,
> 43 until I make your enemies
> a footstool for your feet.'[f]

44 Since Dawud calls the Messiah 'Lord,' how can the Messiah be his son?"
45 When all the people were listening, Isa said to his disciples, 46 "Beware of
the scholars of religion. They parade around in expensive robes, and they love
to be greeted in the markets, occupy positions of honor in the prayer halls,
and sit at the head of banquet tables. 47 Yet they devour widows' property and
then give lengthy prayers for show. They will be punished most severely."

Isa Teaches About Offerings to Allah

21 Isa looked up and watched as rich people placed their offerings in
the temple donation box. 2 He also saw a poor widow put in two small
coins.[g]

---

d 20:28 See Deuteronomy 25:5-6.
e 20:37 Exodus 3:6.
f 20:42-43 Zabur/Psalm 110:1.
g 21:2 *Two small coins*—lit. "two leptas." This was a tiny amount of money, a laborer's wages for about ten minutes of work.

3 Then he said, "Listen to me. That poor widow has actually put in more
than anyone. 4 For they all gave out of their surplus. But she, despite her great
need, gave all she had to live on."

Isa Prophesies

5 Some of his disciples marveled at the temple's beautiful stonework and
decorative offerings. But Isa said, 6 "You notice all these things. But a time is
coming when not a single stone will remain upon another. Every one will be
torn down."

7 So they asked him, "Teacher, when will all this happen? What sign will be
given when this is about to occur?"

8 He replied, "Be careful that you're not deceived. Many people will come
in my name, claiming, 'I'm the one!' or 'The time is near!' Don't follow them.
9 And when you hear of wars and revolutions, don't be alarmed. Such things
must happen first, but the end won't come right after." 10 Then he told them,
"Nations will war against nations and kingdoms against kingdoms. 11 Massive
earthquakes will occur, famine and plague in places, and terrifying events
with great signs from heaven.

12 "However, before all that, you will be seized and persecuted, turned over
to religious tribunals and prisons, and taken away to kings and rulers. This
will happen because of me, 13 and be an opportunity for you to testify. 14 But
determine beforehand not to prepare a defense, 15 for I'll give you such words
and wisdom that none of your opponents will be able to oppose or refute you.
16 However, even your own parents, siblings, relatives, and friends will betray
you. And they'll kill some of you. 17 Because of me, everyone will hate you.
18 But not a hair on your head will be lost.[a] 19 Stand firm, and you will preserve
your soul.

20 "When you see al-Quds surrounded by armies, then you'll know its
destruction has come.[b] 21 People in Judea should flee to the hills. Those in
al-Quds should get out, and those outside should not enter. 22 For those will
be days of vengeance, fulfilling all the Scriptures.[c] 23 How dreadful for women
pregnant or nursing in those days, days of disaster in the land and rage
against this people. 24 They will be killed by the sword or taken captive to
many nations. And al-Quds will be trampled upon by the pagans until their
time is complete.

---

a 21:18 Despite what happens to the physical body in times of persecution, ultimately Isa's faithful followers will be saved and thus lose nothing of eternal value (see 9:24; Matthew 10:28).

b 21:20 This prophesy about al-Quds in verses 20-24 was literally fulfilled in A.D. 70, when the city was destroyed by the Romans under the leadership of the future emperor Titus, son of Emperor Vespasian. These events may foreshadow still future similar events at the end of the age.

c 21:22 See Jeremiah 5:29; Hosea 9:7.

[25] "Signs will appear in the sun, moon, and stars, and earth's peoples will be distressed and perplexed by upheavals of sea and surf.[d] [26] They'll be weak with fear and foreboding over events on earth, as the forces of the heavens are shaken.[e] [27] Then the Son of Man will appear, mighty and glorious, arriving on a cloud.[f] [28] So, when these things begin, stand and look up, for your salvation is coming!"

[29] Then he gave them an illustration. "Think of a fig tree or other trees. [30] When they leaf, you see it for yourselves, and you know that summer is near. [31] Likewise, when you see all these things happening, recognize that the kingdom of Allah is near. [32] I tell you the truth, this generation[g] will not pass away until all these things occur. [33] Heaven and earth will pass away, but my words will never pass away.

[34] "So take care that your hearts not be clouded by indulgence, drunkenness, or life's concerns. Otherwise, that day will strike you unaware, [35] like a trap. For it will engulf everyone living on earth. [36] Therefore, be alert in every moment, and pray for strength to rise above all these things and stand tall before the Son of Man."

[37] So, Isa spent his days teaching in the temple, and would go out to the Mount of Olives in the evenings to spend the night. [38] Then, at dawn, all the people would assemble in the temple to hear him.

Judas Agrees to Betray Isa

22 The Festival of Unleavened Bread, also called the Passover, was approaching.[h] [2] And the head priests and scholars of religion, fearing the people, kept looking for ways to kill Isa.

---

d 21:25 Most interpreters agree that here the focus of the prophecies switches to still future events associated with the coming of the Son of Man and the end of the age. See Isaiah 13:9-10; Joel 2:30-31; Acts 2:19-20; Revelation 6:12-14.

e 21:26 See Haggai 2:6, 21.

f 21:27 See Daniyal/Daniel 7:13-14.

g 21:32 *This generation*—there are three main interpretations of these words: 1) They refer to the generation that will witness all the cosmic cataclysms prophesied above followed by the second coming of Isa al-Masih; 2) It is possible that the correct translation here is "this race." If this is the case, it refers to the Hebrew people persisting to the end; 3) Possibly "this generation" refers to Isa al-Masih's generation which witnessed the destruction of al-Quds in A.D. 70. In this case the words "all these things occur" refer not to events in the last days, but only to the prophesy about al-Quds.

h 22:1 *Festival of Unleavened Bread*—during this seven day long festival the people were to eat unleavened bread (see Exodus 12:15-20; Leviticus 23:6-8; Numbers 28:17-25). *Passover*—this holiday, which directly preceded the Festival of Unleavened Bread, was held to commemorate the deliverance of the Hebrew people from slavery in Egypt under the leadership of Prophet Musa (see Exodus 12:1-14; Numbers 1:14; Deuteronomy 16:1-8). Over time these two holidays essentially merged into one and their names became interchangeable.

[3] Then Shaitan entered into Judas Iscariot, one of the twelve emissaries.
[4] And Judas went and discussed with the head priests and temple guards how
he might betray Isa to them. [5] They were delighted and decided to pay him.
[6] So he agreed, and began looking for an occasion apart from a crowd he could
give them Isa.

Isa Eats His Last Meal

[7] Then the Festival of Unleavened Bread arrived, the day when the Passover
lamb was to be sacrificed. [8] And Isa sent off Peter and John, saying, "Go and
prepare for us the Passover meal."

[9] They asked him, "Where would you like us to do it?"

[10] He replied, "As soon as you enter the city, a man carrying a water jug will
meet you. Follow him to the house he enters. [11] Then say to the home's owner,
'The teacher asks: Where is the guest room for me to eat the Passover with
my disciples?' [12] He will show you a large, furnished upper room. Prepare the
meal there." [13] They left and found everything just as Isa had said. And they
prepared the Passover there.

[14] When the time came, Isa and his emissaries sat down together to eat.
[15] And Isa said to them, "I've been so eager to eat this Passover meal with you
before I suffer. [16] As for me, I won't eat this meal again until its fulfillment in
the kingdom of Allah."

[17] Picking up a full cup he thanked Allah for it and said, "Take this and share
it among yourselves. [18] As for me, I will not drink again from the fruit of the
vine until the kingdom of Allah has come."

[19] Then he took some bread, thanked Allah for it, broke it in pieces, and
gave them to the disciples, saying, "This is my body given for you. Eat this in
remembrance of me."

[20] After the meal he took a full cup and said, "This cup is the new covenant
established in my blood shed for you.[a]

[21] "But here, right at this table with me, is the one who will betray me. [22] The
Son of Man must go the way it was determined. But woe to the one who
betrays him." [23] And the disciples started asking each other which of them
would do such a thing.

[24] Then they began to argue which of them was the greatest. [25] But Isa told
them, "Kings rule over the nations, and people with authority call themselves
benefactors. [26] But you must be different. The greatest among you should
consider themselves the youngest, and the leaders, servants. [27] Who is more
important, a person at the table, or a servant? The one at the table, right? But
I'm here with you as a servant.

[28] "You have stood by me in my difficult trials. [29] So just as my Father has
granted me a kingdom, I grant you the right [30] to eat and drink at my table in
my kingdom. And you'll sit on thrones, judging[b] the twelve tribes of Israel.

---

a 22:20 Compare Exodus 24:8; Hebrews 9:18-20.

b 22:30 Or "ruling over."

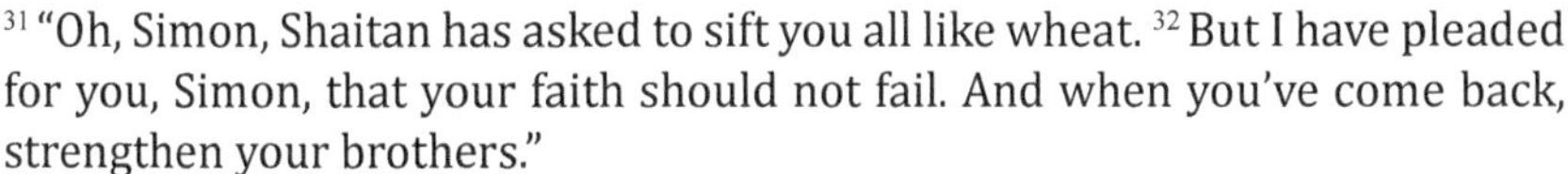

Isa Predicts Peter's Denial

[31] "Oh, Simon, Shaitan has asked to sift you all like wheat. [32] But I have pleaded
for you, Simon, that your faith should not fail. And when you've come back,
strengthen your brothers."

[33] But Peter said to him, "Lord, I'm ready to go with you to prison and to
death."

[34] But Isa said, "Listen to me, Peter. Before the rooster crows today, three
times you will deny knowing me.

[35] "When I sent you out to preach, and had you take along no money, pack,
or extra sandals, did you need anything?"

"No," they replied.

[36] "But now," he said, "take money and a pack. And if you don't have a sword,
sell even your cloak to buy one.[c] [37] Note that this Scripture is about to be
fulfilled in my life: 'He was classified as an anarchist.'[d] Yes, what's written
about me will be fulfilled."

[38] And they replied, "Lord, look. Here are two swords."

And he said, "That's enough."

Isa Prays

[39] Then he left as usual for the Mount of Olives, and his disciples followed.
[40] When they arrived he told them, "Pray that you don't yield to temptation."

[41] He went off about a stone's throw away and knelt in prayer, [42] saying,
"Father, if you are willing, remove this bitter cup from me. But may your
will, not mine, be done." [43] Then an angel from heaven appeared to him and
strengthened him. [44] Agonizing, he prayed even more fervently. And his sweat,
becoming like blood, dripped on the ground.

[45] Then he stood from prayer and went over to the disciples. He found them
asleep, drained by grief. [46] And he asked, "Why are you sleeping? Get up and
pray so you won't yield to temptation."

Isa Is Betrayed and Arrested

[47] As Isa said that, a crowd arrived led by Judas, one of the twelve disciples.
And Judas approached Isa and kissed him. [48] But Isa said, "Judas, is it with a
kiss that you betray the Son of Man?"

[49] When his disciples saw what was happening, they exclaimed, "Lord,
should we strike with the swords!" [50] And one of them did strike, cutting off
the right ear of the high priest's servant.

[51] But Isa said, "Enough of this!" And he touched the man's ear and healed
him.

---

c 22:36 The meaning of this verse is that Isa's followers must prepare themselves to persevere in the upcoming spiritual battle, and to endure loss and persecution for their faith. A literal understanding would be contradictory to what Isa said later that same day (see Matthew 26:51-53; Luke 22:49-51; see also John 18:36; 2 Corinthians 10:3-4).

d 22:37 Isaiah 53:12.

52 Then Isa spoke to the head priests, temple guards, and elders who had
come for him. "Why do you show up with swords and clubs, as if to capture a
revolutionary? 53 Every day I was in the temple with you, but you didn't seize
me there. This is your time, when darkness rules!"

Peter Disowns Isa

54 So they arrested him and took him to the house of the high priest. Peter
followed at a distance. 55 Then some of them lit a fire in the courtyard and sat
around it, Peter among them. 56 As he sat there, a servant girl noticed him in
the firelight. She stared at Peter and said, "This man was with him!"

57 But Peter denied it, saying "Lady, I don't know him!"

58 After a while someone else saw him and said, "You're one of them!"

Peter responded, "Mister, I am not!"

59 About an hour later yet one more person insisted, "This fellow was surely
with him. He's a Galilean, too!"

60 But Peter said, "Mister, I don't know what you're talking about!" Right
then, while he was still speaking, a rooster crowed.

61 And the Lord turned to look at Peter, and Peter remembered what the
Lord had said: "Before the rooster crows today, you will disown me three
times." 62 Then Peter went out and wept bitterly.

63 The men guarding Isa set about mocking and beating him. 64 And they
blindfolded him, saying, "Prophesy! Guess who hit you that time!" 65 And in
many other ways they continued to insult him.

Isa Is on Trial Before the High Council

66 At daybreak the assembly of people's elders—head priests and scholars
of religion—convened. Isa was led before this high council,[a] 67 and they
demanded, "If you are the Messiah, tell us."

But he replied, "If I tell you, you'll never believe it. 68 And if I ask you a
question, you'll never respond. 69 But from now on the Son of Man will be
seated at the right of Allah Almighty!"[b]

70 They all said, "So, you are the Son of the Most High?!"

He replied to them, "You said it. I am."

71 And they responded, "Why do we need other witnesses? We've heard it
ourselves, straight from his own mouth!"

Isa Is on Trial Before Pilate

23 Then the entire council rose, took him to Pilate,[c] 2 and made accusations
against Isa. They said, "We've determined that this man leads our

---

a 22:66 *High council*—lit. "Sanhedrin." The supreme political, religious and judicial body of the Hebrews. The high council consisted of seventy-one men.

b 22:69 Zabur/Psalm 110:1.

c 23:1 Pontius Pilate was the Roman governor in Judah from A.D. 26 to 36.

people astray. He forbids paying taxes to Caesar and proclaims himself
Messiah, a king."[d]
3 So Pilate asked him, "Are you the king of the Jews?"
Isa replied, "Yes, as you say."
4 Then Pilate said to the head priests and the crowd, "I find no case against
this man."
5 But they were insistent, saying. "He incites the people with his teaching—
all over Judea, and from Galilee to here!"
6 When Pilate heard that, he asked whether Isa was a Galilean. 7 Learning
that to be so, Isa therefore being under Herod's[e] jurisdiction, Pilate sent Isa
to him, for Herod was in al-Quds at the time.
8 Herod, for his part, was delighted to see Isa. He had heard about him, and
for a long time had very much hoped to see Isa perform a miracle. 9 So he
asked Isa numerous questions, but Isa made no response. 10 And the head
priests and scholars of religion stood by, accusing Isa vigorously. 11 So Herod
came to despise him, and with his soldiers mocked Isa by dressing him in
luxurious clothes. Then he sent Isa back to Pilate. 12 Herod and Pilate became
friends that day, though they had previously been enemies.
13 Then Pilate called together the head priests, various leaders, and the
people themselves. 14 He told them, "You brought me this man accused of
inciting a revolt. I have examined him in your presence and find no basis for
your case against him. 15 And neither did Herod, so he sent him back to us. He
has committed no crime worthy of death. 16-17 I will therefore punish him and
release him."[f]
18 But the crowd cried out, "Kill him, and release Barabbas for us!"
19 (Barabbas had been imprisoned for a revolt in the city and for murder.)
20 Wanting to release Isa, Pilate addressed them yet again. 21 But they kept
shouting, "Crucify him! Crucify him!"
22 Pilate addressed them a third time. "Why? What crime has he committed?
I've found he's done nothing worthy of death. I will therefore punish him and
release him."
23 But they continued shouting, calling for Isa to be crucified. And their
shouts prevailed. 24 So Pilate consented to their demand— 25 he released the
man they sought, the one imprisoned for revolt and murder, but he delivered
Isa over to their demand.

Isa Is Crucified

26 As Isa was led away, a Cyrenian man named Simon was coming from the
countryside. The soldiers took hold of him, put the cross on him, and forced

---

d 23:2 Isa al-Masih's accusers were willing to tell a bold-faced lie. They accused Isa of forbidding people to pay taxes to the emperor, even though Isa had said exactly the opposite (see 20:22-25).

e 23:7 The reference is to Herod Antipas (see footnote on 3:1).

f 23:16-17 Some manuscripts include verse 17: "Now during the Passover he was obliged to release one of the prisoners." See Matthew 27:15; Mark 15:6.

him to carry it behind Isa. [27] A large crowd followed, with women mourning and weeping. [28] But Isa turned and said to them, "Daughters of al-Quds, don't weep for me. Weep instead for yourselves and your children. [29] For the days are coming when people will say, 'Blessed are the childless, the wombs that never bore a child and the breasts that never fed one!' [30] People will beg the mountains, 'Fall on us!' and the hills, 'Bury us!'[a] [31] If they do such things now to a green tree, what will happen to one that's dried up?"[b]

[32] With him they also led away two criminals for execution. [33] When they arrived at the place called the Skull,[c] they crucified him there. They also crucified the two criminals, one on his right and one on his left.

[34] But Isa said, "Father, forgive them! They don't know what they're doing." And they divided up his clothing by throwing dice.[d]

[35] The people stood by and watched. And the leaders mocked, saying, "He saved others. Now he should save himself—if he's really Allah's Messiah, the Chosen One!"[e] [36] The soldiers also ridiculed him and offered him vinegar to drink.[f] [37] They said, "If you are the king of the Jews, save yourself!" [38] And a sign was fastened above him which read: "The king of the Jews."

[39] One of the criminals hanging beside him jeered, "So you're the Messiah, eh? Save yourself, and us too!"

[40] But the other criminal responded in rebuke, "Have you no fear of Allah, even when sentenced to the same? [41] We deserve what we got—justice for our crimes. But this man has done nothing wrong." [42] Then he said, "Isa, remember me when you come into your kingdom."

[43] And Isa replied, "I promise you, today you'll be with me in Paradise."

Isa Dies

[44] At about noon deep darkness descended over the whole land, and it lasted until three o'clock. [45] The sun ceased to shine, and the curtain in the temple ripped down the middle.[g] [46] Then Isa shouted, "Father, I entrust my spirit to your care!"[h] With that he breathed his last.

[47] When the military officer saw what had happened, he glorified Allah, saying, "This man was truly innocent!" [48] And when the crowds which had gathered to watch saw what happened, they returned home grief-stricken.

a 23:30 Hosea 10:8; compare also Revelation 6:16.
b 23:31 Here the green tree probably symbolizes Isa's righteousness while the dry tree refers to the spiritual condition of sinful people (compare Ezekiel 20:45–21:7).
c 23:33 Probably the form of the hill gave rise to this name because it resembled a human skull.
d 23:34 See Zabur/Psalm 22:18.
e 23:35 See Zabur/Psalm 22:6-8.
f 23:36 See Zabur/Psalm 69:21.
g 23:45 This was the interior curtain in the temple that separated the "Holy Place" from the "Holy of Holies" (see Exodus 26:31-35). This event announces that, thanks to Isa's purifying sacrifice, his followers now have direct access to the presence of Allah (see Hebrews 10:19-22).
h 23:46 See Zabur/Psalm 31:5.

49 Those who knew Isa, including the women who followed him from Galilee,
had been standing at a distance to watch.

Isa Is Buried

50 There was a good and upright man named Yusuf. Though a member of the
high council, 51 he was not in agreement with its decision or actions. He lived
in the Judean town of Arimathea, and looked forward to the kingdom of Allah.
52 And so, he went to Pilate and claimed Isa's body. 53 Then he took it down
from the cross, wrapped it in linen cloth, and laid it in a tomb which had
never been used, cut out of rock. 54 It was late Friday, Preparation Day, and the
Day of Rest was about to start.[i]

55 The women who had come with Isa from Galilee followed behind and
watched as his body was placed in the tomb. 56 Then they left and prepared
burial spices and perfumes. And when the Day of Rest started they rested, in
keeping with the commandment.

Isa Returns to Life

24 Very early Sunday morning, the first day of the week, the women went
to the tomb, taking the spices they'd prepared. 2 They saw the stone
rolled away from the entrance. 3 They went in, but didn't find the body of the
Lord Isa. 4 As they were puzzling over that, two men[j] wearing dazzling clothes
appeared to them.

5 The women were afraid and bowed with their faces to the ground. And the
men said, "Why do you seek the living among the dead? 6 He isn't here. He has
returned to life! Remember what he told you back in Galilee? 7 He said that
the Son of Man had to be handed over to sinful people and crucified. And on
the third day he would return to life."

8 Then they remembered Isa's words. 9 So they returned from the tomb
and reported it to the eleven disciples and all the others. 10 The women were
Maryam from Magdala, Joanna, Maryam the mother of Yaqub, and several
others. When they told the emissaries what had happened, 11 it struck them
as nonsense, and they didn't believe it. 12 But Peter got up and ran to the tomb.
Stooping, he looked in and saw the linen wrappings lying by themselves.
Then he went home, marveling at what had happened.

Isa Joins Men Walking

13 That same day two of Isa's followers were going to Emmaus, a village
about eleven kilometers[k] from al-Quds. 14 They talked with each other about
everything that had happened. 15 And while they talked and discussed these

---

i 23:54 The Sabbath, the religious Day of Rest on which the Hebrews were not allowed to do any kind of work, began on Friday with the setting of the sun. This was the reason for Isa's hurried burial.

j 24:4 *Two men*—i.e., angels (see 24:23).

k 24:13 *Eleven kilometers*—lit. "sixty stadia" or about seven miles.

things, Isa came up and went along with them. [16] But they were prevented from recognizing him.

[17] Then he asked them, "What's this you're discussing so intently as you walk along?"

They stopped, dejected. [18] Then one of them, Cleopas, said to him, "You must be the only person in al-Quds who doesn't know what happened there the last few days."

[19] "What?" Isa asked.

"Things concerning Isa of Nazareth," they replied. "He was a mighty prophet in word and deed, both in the eyes of Allah and people. [20] But our head priests and leaders handed him over to death and crucified him. [21] We had hoped he was the one coming to rescue Israel. But now it's already the third day since that happened.

[22] "However, some women from our group amazed us. They were at his tomb early today, [23] and didn't see his body. They returned reporting they'd seen a vision—angels who said he is alive! [24] Some of those among us then went to see the tomb, and they found it just as the women had said—but his body was gone!"

[25] Then Isa said to them, "Oh, you're so foolish and your hearts are so slow to believe all that the prophets said! [26] Wasn't it necessary for the Messiah to suffer all these things and then enter into his glory?" [27] Then Isa explained to them everything the Scriptures say about himself—what Musa and all the prophets wrote.

[28] As they neared the village where they were heading, Isa seemed as if he were going on ahead. [29] But they pleaded with him, "Stay with us! It's getting late and the day's almost over." So he went in and stayed with them. [30] And when he sat down with them to eat, he took the bread, blessed it, broke it, and gave it to them. [31] Then their eyes were opened and they recognized him, and he disappeared.

[32] They said to each other, "As he talked along on the way, explaining the Scriptures to us, wasn't it as if our hearts were on fire?" [33] And within the hour they set out back to al-Quds. There they found the eleven disciples and the others with them, [34] who told the two, "The Lord has really risen! And he appeared to Simon!"

Isa Appears to the Disciples

[35] Then the two explained what happened on the road and how they recognized Isa when he broke the bread. [36] And just as they were talking about it, Isa himself appeared, standing among them. "Peace to you!"[a] he said. [37] They were startled and afraid, thinking it was a ghost.

[38] But he said to them, "Why are you troubled? Why are your hearts filled with doubt? [39] Look at my hands and my feet. It's me! Touch me. See—ghosts

---

a 24:36 *Peace to you!*—in the Hebrew language this phrase is pronounced *shalom aleichem* and is closely related to the Arabic greeting *as-salamu alaykum*.

don't have flesh and bones like I do!" [40] As he spoke, he showed them his
hands and feet.
[41] While they were still in disbelief from joy and amazement, he asked them,
"Do you have anything here to eat?" [42] So they gave him a piece of broiled fish.
[43] And as they watched, he took it and ate it.
[44] Then he said to them, "I told you this before when I was with you—
that everything written about me in the law of Musa, the Prophets, and the
Zabur must be fulfilled." [45] Then he opened their minds to understand the
Scriptures. [46] He said, "This was written—that the Messiah would suffer and
die, and return to life from death on the third day [47] —and that forgiveness
of sins for all who repent should be proclaimed in his name to all peoples,
beginning in al-Quds. [48] You are witnesses of these things.
[49] "And listen, I will send to you what my Father promised. So stay in the city
until you are clothed with power from Heaven."

Isa Ascends to Heaven

[50] Then Isa led them to Bethany. And lifting up his hands, he blessed them.
[51] While he was blessing them, he departed from them and was taken up into
heaven. [52] They worshiped him, and then returned to al-Quds with great joy.
[53] And they spent all of their time in the temple, praising Allah.

Topical Articles

Did Isa al-Masih Really Die Like the Holy Scriptures Say? Part One

Yes, Isa died. Allah often allows people the great honor of being martyred for their faith. But Isa is far greater than a typical martyr. Not only was he killed for teaching the truth, death was his mission in life. On this the Scriptures are very clear. Isa said about himself:

> *"Kings rule over the nations, and people with authority call themselves benefactors. But you must be different. The greatest among you should consider themselves the youngest, and the leaders, servants. Who is more important, a person at the table, or a servant? The one at the table, right? But I'm here with you as a servant."*
>
> (Luke 22:25-27)

Isa also said:

> *"The Son of Man did not come to be served but to serve, and to give up his life as a ransom for many."*
>
> (Matthew 20:28)

And just before his death, he also said:

> *"I tell you the solemn truth, unless a kernel of wheat falls into the ground and dies, it remains by itself alone. But if it dies, it produces much grain. The one who loves his life destroys it, and the one who hates his life in this world guards it for eternal life. If anyone wants to serve me, he must follow me, and where I am, my servant will be too. If anyone serves me, the Father will honor him. Now my soul is greatly distressed. And what should I say? 'Father, deliver me from this hour'? No, but for this very reason I have come to this hour."*
>
> (John 12:24-27, NET)

The great prophet Isaiah, inspired by Allah hundreds of years before Isa lived on earth, wrote this profound prophecy about the Messiah who would come:

> *See, my servant will act wisely; he will be raised and lifted up and highly exalted. Just as there were many who were appalled at him—his appearance was so disfigured beyond that of any human being and his form marred beyond human likeness—so he will sprinkle many nations, and kings will shut their mouths because of him. For what they were not told, they will see, and what they have not heard,*

> *they will understand. Who has believed our message and to whom has the arm of the LORD been revealed? He grew up before him like a tender shoot, and like a root out of dry ground. He had no beauty or majesty to attract us to him, nothing in his appearance that we should desire him. He was despised and rejected by mankind, a man of suffering, and familiar with pain. Like one from whom people hide their faces he was despised, and we held him in low esteem. Surely he took up our pain and bore our suffering, yet we considered him punished by God, stricken by him, and afflicted. But he was pierced for our transgressions, he was crushed for our iniquities; the punishment that brought us peace was on him, and by his wounds we are healed. We all, like sheep, have gone astray, each of us has turned to our own way; and the LORD has laid on him the iniquity of us all. He was oppressed and afflicted, yet he did not open his mouth; he was led like a lamb to the slaughter, and as a sheep before its shearers is silent, so he did not open his mouth. By oppression and judgment he was taken away. Yet who of his generation protested? For he was cut off from the land of the living; for the transgression of my people he was punished. He was assigned a grave with the wicked, and with the rich in his death, though he had done no violence, nor was any deceit in his mouth. Yet it was the LORD's will to crush him and cause him to suffer, and though the LORD makes his life an offering for sin, he will see his offspring and prolong his days, and the will of the LORD will prosper in his hand. After he has suffered, he will see the light of life and be satisfied; by his knowledge my righteous servant will justify many, and he will bear their iniquities. Therefore I will give him a portion among the great, and he will divide the spoils with the strong, because he poured out his life unto death, and was numbered with the transgressors. For he bore the sin of many, and made intercession for the transgressors.*
>
> (Isaiah 52:13–53:12, NIV)

As the prophet said, "After he has suffered, he will see the light of life." The Gospels clearly tell us that three days after Isa died,[a] he came back to life. That seems impossible, but nothing is impossible with Allah. At first even Isa's followers did not believe it had happened. But he showed himself to them alive. Then they believed, they traveled about and preached the good news of forgiveness through Isa's sacrificial death, and they were killed like their Master.

No one but Allah could imagine a person like Isa al-Masih. He is the ultimate sacrifice for all people. Animals are not good enough. Isa was sinless, and for that reason, he was the perfect sacrifice.

---

a He died on Friday, and came back to life on Sunday. By their phraseology, it was "three days later," or "on the third day."

> *Therefore, since we have a great high priest who has entered heaven, Isa the Son of the Most High, we should firmly hold to the faith we profess. And our high priest is not one who is unable to sympathize with our weaknesses. In fact, he was tempted in every way like we are, yet he never sinned.*
>
> (Hebrews 4:14-15)

> *Therefore, whoever has a relationship with the Messiah is a new creation. The former things have passed away; new things have come! And all this is from Allah, who has restored our relationship to him through the Messiah and has given to us the task of restoration. Specifically, Allah was in the Messiah restoring the world to himself, not counting people's sins immoral actions against them. And he has entrusted to us this message of restoration. So we are the Messiah's ambassadors, Allah making his appeal through us. On the Messiah's behalf, we implore you to be restored to Allah. He made the One who never sinned sinful on our behalf so that through him we might share Allah's moral purity.*
>
> (2 Corinthians 5:17-21)

With or without faith, we will experience difficulty in life. No difficulty is so great that it should keep us from seeking and believing the truth. When you think about truth, consider Isa al-Masih.

(For more, see the article titled, "Why Do We Need a Sacrifice? Can't Allah Just Forgive?")

Did Isa al-Masih Really Die Like the Holy Scriptures Say? Part Two

The physical damage inflicted upon Isa's body strongly points to death:

1. Isa was severely whipped, beaten, and crucified.
2. Soldiers stuck him in the side with a spear.
3. Water and blood came out of the spear hole (itself proof of severe internal damage).
4. Those who buried Isa's body wrapped it in tight cloths.
5. He was put in a cold rock tomb sealed with a great rock and guarded by soldiers.
6. Despite agonizing torture and great loss of bodily fluids, he had nothing to drink for many hours.

Any one of those things could kill a person. Taken together, surviving such treatment would require a miracle. Though Isa had performed many miracles upon others, he never spoke about escaping death. On the contrary, he said he came to die and would certainly be killed. The testimonies about Isa's death are strong, diverse, and consistent:

7. The soldiers who crucified him believed he died. They knew death when they saw it.
8. The Roman governor Pilate was convinced that Isa had died.
9. The historical accounts of observers—Matthew, John, and Mark—state that he died.
10. Luke, a physician and proven historian, interviewed many people and wrote about Isa and his death.
11. Isa's other disciples and followers believed that he had died.
12. First and second century secular writers (e.g., Josephus, Tacitus, Lucian) speak of Isa's death.

You are encouraged to read the Gospel accounts themselves. See Matthew chapters 26-28, Mark chapters 14-16, Luke chapters 22-24 and John chapters 18-21. They tell not only of Isa's death, but also his resurrection. Multiple accounts provide tremendous historical substantiation. Finally, there are also the important words of Isa's emissary Paul:

> *Now, brothers and sisters, I spell out for you the good news which I proclaimed to you. It's what you accepted, on which you stake your lives, and through which you are saved. (Assuming you firmly hold to the message I proclaimed to you. Otherwise, your faith was not real.) I received what is paramount and passed it on to you. Specifically, the*

> *Messiah died for our sins, as the Scriptures foretold. He was buried but on the third day he returned to life, as the Scriptures foretold. After that he appeared to Peter and then to the twelve emissaries. Then he appeared to more than 500 of his disciples at one time. (Most of them are still living, though some have died.) Later, he appeared to Yaqub, and then to all his emissaries. Last of all, as if to someone born unexpectedly, he appeared also to me.*
>
> (1 Corinthians 15:1-8)

Many people, both from the time of Isa and soon thereafter, have spoken. Their testimony cannot be simply negated by anyone born centuries later.

How Can Isa Be the "Son of the Most High"?

Before we explore this topic, we should readily acknowledge that it is extremely controversial, and for many people emotionally upsetting. This subject is best approached after preparatory prayer. Many believe that the Injil just could not be saying what it seems to be saying. And yet, there are no manuscripts of the Injil which could be construed so as to avoid these implications. Those who believe "it must have been changed," have absolutely no manuscript evidence on which to base their claim. If we value the truth, we need to look at the evidence as it is, not as we wish it to be.

A zealous religious man approached his friend, a follower of Isa al-Masih.

Religious man: "Isa was a great prophet—but only a human being."

Follower of Isa: "Is Allah all-powerful and is anything possible for him?"

Religious man: "Yes, of course!"

Follower of Isa: "Then couldn't the Most High come to earth in human form?"

However, saying that Allah could come to earth is not the same as saying that he did. Did our Creator, in fact, come to earth in human form? That's the question we will explore below.

First, the expression "son of" does not always refer to the child of a man and a woman. Isa called two of his disciples "sons of thunder" (Mark 3:17). And he told some self-righteous Hebrews that their father was Iblis (John 8:44). Obviously this is figurative language: Isa didn't mean that thunder or Iblis had slept with women. Likewise, devout Hebrews of Isa's day sometimes called Allah their "Father," but they never dreamed that this implied Allah had literal offspring. Some languages even today use the expression "son of" to describe a person's character.

What about Isa? Did he claim to be "the Son of God"? Yes. On that Isa was very clear. Note these important verses from the Gospels of John and of Luke.

> *"So how can you claim that I—the one whom the Father sanctified and sent into the world—that I blaspheme by calling myself 'the Son of the Most High'? If I don't perform my Father's deeds, then don't believe me. But if I do, even if you don't believe in me, believe in the works themselves. Then you'll know and understand that the Father is in me and I am in the Father."*
>
> (John 10:36-38)

Isa continued, "My Father entrusted everything to me. No one knows the Son except the Father, or the Father except the Son—and anyone to whom the Son chooses to reveal him."

(Luke 10:22)

In what sense could this mean that Isa is God's "Son"?

1. In a general sense, the Holy Scriptures speak of Allah as the "Father" of all true believers, for he gives us new spiritual life (John 1:12-13). In that sense all true believers are Allah's "children," adopted into his spiritual family (Galatians 4:4-7). But this does not apply to the One we now call Isa, for he already existed before he came to earth (John 1:1-4, 14; John 8:48-59; Galatians 4:4).
2. In ancient Israel, the king on Dawud's throne was considered Allah's vice-regent on earth and called his son (2 Samuel 7:14). Coronation was described metaphorically as the Most High "begetting" a son, (Zabur/Psalm 2:6-7). Isa is certainly called "Son of the Most High" in this sense, as such he is indeed the Messiah, the Son of God, now enthroned at the right hand of the Most High (Luke 1:32-33; John 1:49; Acts 13:32-33; Hebrews 1:3-5).
3. But Isa was special in another way. Aside from the first man, Adam, whom Allah made from earth, Isa is the only human being to not have an earthly father. As described in Luke 1:34-35, his mother conceived as a virgin through a miraculous, non-sexual act of Allah's Holy Spirit. So, in this sense also Isa can be called the "Son of the Most High." No true follower of Isa believes that God Almighty had relations with Maryam, and clearly the Injil does not teach such a thing. It should never be made a point of debate, and attempts to do so are either foolish or ill-intended.
4. The Jews believed in only one God as strongly as any people ever has. When Isa used Father/Son terminology to express his unique relationship with the Most High, the religious leaders accused him of blasphemy for making himself equal with God (Luke 22:70-71; John 5:17-18; 10:30-33, 36). Neither Isa, who died for this assertion, nor the authors of the Injil, ever denied his equality with God (Luke 22:70; John 10:28-29; 19:7, Romans 9:5; 2 Peter 1:1; Revelation 5:11-14). So, in calling Isa the "Son of the Most High," the Injil, however shockingly, asserts his deity.

But how can Isa be divine? If that were true, wouldn't it mean there is more than one God? Isn't that shirk and the worst kind of blasphemy?!

Those are excellent questions, and we'll address them in the next section.

How Can Isa Be Divine? How Can Allah, Who Is One, Be a "Trinity"?—Part One

Experience has shown that, until a person acknowledges their need for a savior, they seldom are ready to consider the possibility, let alone be convinced, that Isa is God or that Allah is a trinity. On the other hand, once a person sees the enormity of their own sin and understands the holiness and justice of the almighty God, they not only understand that they need a savior, but that the savior must be divine. At that point, people seldom if ever have trouble with the doctrine of the trinity as taught in all the ancient manuscripts of the Holy Scriptures. So, read this article with these thoughts in mind!

If Isa were God, wouldn't it mean there is more than one God? Isn't that shirk and the worst kind of blasphemy? (As for Isa being both human and divine, see the discussion about what the Injil really means when it calls Isa the Son of the Most High.)

To answer these important questions, let's back up and look at ourselves. In addition to our bodies, we have invisible elements that include a soul and a spirit. Our spirit makes us alive yet differs from that of animals. We also have a mind, will, emotions and conscience, all parts of our soul. With that come memory, wishes, desires, and more. Removing any aspect will severely damage or even destroy a person.

If we are complicated beings, how much more so Allah ta'ala who made us?

Imagine you are at your daughter's wedding. You are sad that you'll see less of her, but happy for her new life. You are satisfied that you raised her to be a good wife and mother. You trust that your son-in-law will be a good provider, but you still worry about the new couple's finances, so you make plans to help them. You expect them to have children of their own. You anticipate the joy of becoming a grandparent. You wonder how things will go with the other set of grandparents.

If, in such a situation, we can discern within ourselves more than one set of reactions, thoughts or emotions, might that reflect something of the nature of God? Surely he's not less complex than we are. The Holy Scriptures teach that Allah is all-powerful (omnipotent), all-knowing (omniscient), and everywhere at once (omnipresent). He is kind and compassionate, yet also a stern judge of evil. In fact, Allah's characteristics, and thus his "names," are inexhaustible. Ninety-nine names, even nine hundred and ninety-nine, do not suffice to describe him.

In Genesis, the first book of the Holy Scriptures, we read that Allah made people in his own "likeness."

So Allah created man like himself,
in the likeness of God he created them.
Male and female he created them.

(Genesis 1:27)

Of course this cannot mean Allah has a body, but that we are like him in important ways. He doesn't have a mouth or ears as we do, but he can communicate. He never does what is wrong, but like us he knows the difference between the two. And because he loves and cares for us weak and sinful creatures, he is compassionate. That means that Allah has emotions. Allah is complex.

Let's look at things from another direction. Before Allah created anything, with whom did he communicate? What was there to choose from which could be either right or wrong? How could Allah show love and care? If, before anything else existed, Allah was a one-in-one, solitary being—like a single person on a desert island in a vast ocean—then he could make noise but not communicate, he could act but do no right or wrong, and though he might feel love, there would be no one upon whom to bestow it. If that were the situation, Allah would need beings like us in order to express himself. He would need to create in order to be fulfilled. Now that is blasphemous.

Allah is self-existent. He is happy and fulfilled in and by himself. He needs no one and nothing. But how could that be when he was alone, surrounded by an ocean of nothingness? That's where the hint of our own nature, above, comes in. We consist of interacting spiritual parts which reflect, somehow, the essence of Allah. This points to a deep mystery we dare not miss. To get a glimpse of it, let's look further at Isa.

How Can Isa Be Divine? How Can Allah, Who Is One, Be a "Trinity"?—Part Two

The Holy Scriptures say that in the beginning Allah spoke and things came into being (Genesis 1-2). They also say this:

> *In the very beginning was the Word. The Word was with God and was God. He was in the beginning with God. Everything was made through him. Not a single created thing was made apart from him. ... And the Word became a human being and lived among us.*
>
> (John 1:1-3, 14)

People who believe in the Holy Scriptures believe in only one God. But what is the nature of God? If our own nature is complex and mysterious, how much more is Allah's. If we have parts that interrelate and communicate, what about him? Isa came to earth as a man, but before that he was the Word of God. In the beginning, Allah's command brought everything into being (Hebrews 11:3). God's Word has power. How that can be we don't know, any more than we know all about ourselves. Allah ta'ala is more complex than we realize.

The word "trinity" is not in the Holy Scriptures, but the concept is. Just prior to leaving earth and returning to heaven, Isa told his followers to ritually wash new disciples "in the name of the Father and the Son and Allah's Holy Spirit." Isa said "name," not "names." In other places he claimed very boldly to be one with God (e.g., John 10:22-39). Likewise, Allah's Holy Spirit is called God (e.g., Acts 5:3-4). So the Scriptures teach that there is one God consisting of three persons, each of whom can separately be called "God" because they are of the divine essence. This is the doctrine of the trinity.

When Isa claimed to be the Son of the Most High, he was not implying that he was created through Maryam, his earthly mother. She was only the means by which the eternal Word of God came into this world. The Word of God is one of the titles of Isa from eternity, according to John 1:1-4, 14. Before that time he was one with Allah. Allah did not need to create anything because he was not a one-in-one being. He was self-sufficient and self-fulfilled, a three-in-one being consisting of the Father, his Son (also known as his Word), and his Holy Spirit. Within his own self, Allah could communicate, love, and do what was right. He was and remains content and self-fulfilled, able to fully function apart from anyone else. He created because love shares, and he wanted to share his love with us. These are deep truths, but ones that should not shock us. Anything less takes away from Allah's power, his grandeur, his majesty, and his infinitude. Allah is great, and far greater than we imagine. The Scriptures do not try to fully explain the mystery of God's nature or how he came to earth. How can a mere man understand Allah? The Scriptures simply state the truth.

Beyond all question, the mystery from which true godliness springs is great:

He appeared in a body,
was vindicated by the Spirit,
was seen by angels,
was preached among the nations,
was believed on in the world,
was taken up in glory.

(1 Timothy 3:16, NIV)

Embrace the attitude of Isa al-Masih. Though fully divine, he did not cling to equality with the Most High. Instead, he set his glory aside and became a servant, fully human. And when he was a man, he obeyed and humbled himself unto death, and that on a cross. Therefore Allah has greatly honored him, granting him a name above all others. So, at the name of Isa, every knee will bow, whether in high heaven, upon the earth, or beneath it all, and every mouth will acknowledge that Isa Masih is Lord, to the glory of God the Father.

(Philippians 2:5-11)

An example from the physical world might help, although no analogy is really sufficient to describe the magnificence of the Most High. We all know about fire. It cooks our meals and warms our homes. A giant fire in space lights up our world. We speak of "fire" as a single thing, but it actually consists of three elements: a fuel source, a visible flame, and heat. Remove any one and there can be no fire. Three elements, one concept, one word. Fire points to the trinity. God the Father is like the fuel. Isa, coming from him, said "I am the light of the world" (John 8:12). The Holy Spirit, like the invisible heat, brings Allah's power to the world and even to a person's life (Ephesians 5:9; Galatians 5:22-23). Maybe that's why Allah first spoke to the great prophet Musa through a fire, a burning bush that was not consumed (Exodus 3:1-6).

There is only one God. He is one and three-in-one. He is great, and his nature is marvelous.

What About Food and Drink? Are Some Things Forbidden or Not?

The Holy Scriptures say a lot about food. But before discussing dietary restrictions, we should first ask about Allah's general purposes for food.

There are many ways to approach this topic. We all know the pleasures related to eating. Good food is enjoyable, for Allah intended it that way. As the Injil says:

> *It was Allah who created various foods, so those who know and believe the truth can eat them with gratitude. ... Allah richly provides us everything to enjoy.*
>
> (1 Timothy 4:3, 6:17)

Dining with friends and family multiplies the enjoyment, something Isa also appreciated. All this demonstrates Allah's goodness.

Food also demonstrates our dependence upon Allah. This thought should make us humble and turn us away from pride. Prophet Musa noted these truths when he reminded the Israelites of Allah's guidance in their lives:

> *So he humbled you by making you hungry and then feeding you with unfamiliar manna. He did this to teach you that humankind cannot live by bread alone, but also by everything that comes from the Lord's mouth.*
>
> (Deuteronomy 8:3, NET)

For all this, Allah deserves our praise.

Those are the central concepts that have been clear from the beginning. At times, however, Allah has changed the rules about eating. Adam and Hawwa were vegetarians (Genesis 1:29-30). Later, Allah told Prophet Nuh he could also eat any animal, but not blood (Genesis 9:3-4). Later still, through Prophet Musa, Allah gave very strict dietary regulations to the nation of Israel. That helped make them distinct as his special people. But Allah also intended that those religious laws create certain problems. He wanted the Israelites to learn that no one was perfect—that no one could do all Allah required (Acts 15:10; Galatians 4:1–5:3). Later, when Isa al-Masih lived on earth, he once again declared that any food could be eaten without fear of breaking Allah's rules.

> *He said to them, "Are you so foolish? Don't you understand that whatever goes into a person from outside cannot defile him? For it does not enter his heart but his stomach, and then goes out into the sewer." (This means all foods are clean.) He said, "What comes out of a*

> *person defiles him. For from within, out of the human heart, come evil ideas, sexual immorality, theft, murder, adultery, greed, evil, deceit, debauchery, envy, slander, pride, and folly. All these evils come from within and defile a person."*
>
> (Mark 7:18-23, NET)

To reinforce that teaching, Allah gave a special vision to Peter, using him to convey the truth to the then largely Hebrew community of believers (Acts 10:1-48, 15:1-31).

Sadly, instead of uniting all people in appreciation for and dependence upon Allah, our beliefs about food often divide us. True believers in Allah are more concerned with others than with their own diet. They set aside their natural preferences and social practices in order to love others (1 Corinthians 8:1-13). We need to probe the motivations behind our dietary habits. When it comes to food, we humans can be tremendous hypocrites. If our choice of diet makes us proud, we are hurting not only others, but we damage our own relationship with Allah. As Isa's great emissary Paul said:

> *The one who eats everything must not treat with contempt the one who does not, and the one who does not eat everything must not judge the one who does, for God has accepted them.*
>
> (Romans 14:3)

There is also the issue of health. Some of us can't tolerate certain foods and we should avoid them. More often, however, we lack self-control and eat poorly or in excess, turning Allah's gifts into an expression of selfishness and even a means of personal suffering.

Finally, the Injil says that we will eat in heaven (Luke 14:15; Revelation 19:9). Hooray! There, food will never be misused again. Allah has the best ideas.

What About Alcohol? Is That Forbidden?

If alcohol is inherently sinful, then we all have a problem. It's a well-known medical fact that microorganisms in the human digestive system turn some of our food into alcohol—the equivalent of two glasses of wine a day. So we all have some alcohol in our blood all the time. In response to that, someone might claim that the body's internal functions are irrelevant, and that only our purposeful actions matter. There's some truth to that, but when it comes to alcohol, the Holy Scriptures are somewhere in the middle.

On the positive side, Isa himself miraculously turned water into wine at a wedding celebration (John 2:1-11). He would never have done so if alcohol were a sinful substance never to be consumed. Alcohol acts as a preservative, so wine is to fruit juice as yoghurt or cheese is to milk.

However, as with food, moderation is essential. The Holy Scriptures are clearly opposed to both drunkenness and gluttony. What's more, it may be that the unique physical nature of some people predisposes them to intoxication, just like some people are predisposed to gaining excess weight. Each of those two groups should be careful. We cannot live without food, but we can live without drinking alcohol. Others refrain from alcohol as an example of self-control. But whether we drink moderately or abstain entirely, we should not be proud. Personal desires are secondary. Primary should be our desire to glorify Allah and demonstrate his love for others. As Paul said:

> *So then, when you eat, drink, or whatever you do, do it all to glorify Allah. Don't carelessly offend Jews, non-Jews, or Allah's followers. I myself try to be acceptable to everyone in every way. I don't seek what benefits me but what benefits many others, that they might be saved. Imitate me, just as I imitate al-Masih.*
>
> (1 Corinthians 10:31–11:1)

We might note two additional admonitions given by Paul:

> *Do not get drunk with wine, for that leads to recklessness. Instead, be filled with the Spirit, sharing psalms, hymns, and holy songs with one another, singing praises in your hearts to the Lord, and giving thanks always to Allah our heavenly Father in the name of our Lord Isa al-Masih.*
>
> (Ephesians 5:18-20)

> *... to Timothy, my genuine child in the faith. ... Stop drinking just water, but use a little wine for your digestion and your frequent illnesses.*
>
> (1 Timothy 1:2; 5:23, NET)

Finally, we should note the words of Isa:

> *... the mouth speaks about whatever fills the heart. A good person brings out good from the good stored within, and an evil person brings out evil from the evil stored within. Listen to me, on the Day of Judgment people will give an account for every useless thing they have said. For by your words you will be acquitted and by your words you will be condemned.*
>
> (Matthew 12:34-37)

So we see that what comes out of our mouths is of far greater importance than what goes in.

How Can I Be Sure I Will Go to Paradise?

Death exposes the human heart. Note what was said during Isa's crucifixion. The events of that historic time proclaim truth for us all.

> *With him they also led away two criminals for execution. When they arrived at the place called The Skull, they crucified him there. They also crucified the two criminals, one on his right and one on his left.*
>
> *But Isa said, "Father, forgive them! They don't know what they're doing." And they divided up his clothing by throwing dice.*
>
> *The people stood by and watched. And the leaders mocked, saying, "He saved others. Now he should save himself—if he's really Allah's Messiah, the Chosen One!" The soldiers also ridiculed him and offered him vinegar to drink. They said, "If you are the king of the Jews, save yourself!" And a sign was fastened above him which read: "The king of the Jews."*
>
> *One of the criminals hanging beside him jeered, "So you're the Messiah, eh? Save yourself, and us too!"*
>
> *But the other criminal responded in rebuke, "Have you no fear of Allah, even when sentenced to the same? We deserve what we got—justice for our crimes. But this man has done nothing wrong." Then he said, "Isa, remember me when you come into your kingdom."*
>
> *And Isa replied, "I promise you, today you'll be with me in Paradise."*
>
> (Luke 23:32-43)

Though murdered by evil men, Isa died according to the eternal plan of God omnipotent. Cruel people, both Hebrews and pagans, mocked him with delight. Rather than cursing them, Isa prayed they be forgiven. He came for that very reason, a sacrifice for us all.

At the climax of a lifetime's interaction with sinners, we see Isa between two criminals. One joins the mockers and dies with his sins. The other admits his guilt, acknowledges Isa's majesty and seeks his mercy. An aloof sovereign might well ignore such a request from so despicable a subject. But we are all guilty, and King Isa shows mercy to all. Only one thing remains. Like the repentant criminal, we must put our last and only hope in the king. Note what Isa declared:

> *"I am the bread of life. Whoever comes to me will never go hungry, and whoever believes in me will never be thirsty. ... All those the Father gives me will come to me, and whoever comes to me I will never drive away. For I have come down from heaven not to do my will but to do*

the will of him who sent me. And this is the will of him who sent me, that I shall lose none of all those he has given me, but raise them up at the last day. For my Father's will is that everyone who looks to the Son and believes in him shall have eternal life, and I will raise them up at the last day."

(John 6:35, 37-40, NIV)

As one who gives away all his food, so Isa sacrificed his body. No mere human effort compares. Nothing we sinners might do can erase our past, meet Allah's holy demands, and usher us into heaven. But if we turn to Isa, he will never send us away. We can be sure of Paradise simply because only he can offer such a gift, and only he can keep such a promise.

Formerly, you were dead because of your immoral behavior and sins. Engrossed in them, you went about following the ways of this world, the ways of the ruler whose regime occupies our very air, the spirit who even now energizes people who disobey Allah. At one time we all carried on with them, driven by our physical cravings, fulfilling the desires of body and mind. By nature we were just like all the others, destined for punishment. But Allah, who is so abundantly merciful, and because of his great love for us even when we were dead from all our immoralities, he brought us to life with the Messiah. It is his unmerited kindness that has saved us. Allah also raised us up and gave us a place in heaven with Isa al-Masih. He did it all so that in the ages to come he might show us the immense wealth of his gracious, unmerited kindness through Isa al-Masih. So it's by his unmerited kindness you have been saved through faith. It's not of your own doing, but the gift of Allah. It's not by human effort, so that no one can boast.

(Ephesians 2:1-9)

How Should We Understand Gender, Marriage and Family?

Allah created both male and female "in his own image" (Genesis 1:27, NET). So aspects of men and women equally reflect part of the Creator's nature. He is strong yet gentle, he defends and he nurtures, he is independent and social. In short, Allah is like both a good father and a good mother.

Furthermore, though the male was created first, and though men are physically stronger and often called to roles of religious, social, and economic leadership, in heaven marriage will disappear. There both men and women will become glorious angel-like beings (Matthew 22:30). For that reason, even here on earth, men and women are to Allah of equal value (Galatians 3:26-29). Isa showed mercy to repentant prostitutes (Luke 7:40-50; John 8:1-11) and even honored one (Matthew 26:13), but he was very harsh toward arrogant religious men (Matthew 23).

Going back again to the beginning, Allah made one man and one woman. That was his intent for marriage and sexual relations. During the years that followed, some believing men like Ibrahim, Yaqub, Dawud, and Samson had more than one woman or wife. But that was not Allah's intent, and such practices invariably involved trouble and sorrow. Isa al-Masih is clear about all this (Matthew 19:3-12).

Being so basic to creation, marriage and family are two of Allah's greatest gifts to us. The marriage bed is a wondrous and honorable thing (Hebrews 13:4), a near inexplicable physical and emotional unity where two become one in body and heart (Matthew 19:5-6). Another result, should Allah be so gracious, is the miraculous advent of children, new lives given to reflect, bless, and be blessed by the ones who brought them into being.

The world, damaged by sin, is not an easy place. For that reason, the great preacher tells how "two are better than one" (Ecclesiastes 4:9-12). Marriage was Allah's plan before mankind fell into sin, and it remains his plan now. Because it is so important, and because we sinful people are so easily tempted to destroy his great gift, to protect us, Allah has much to say about protecting marriage. His design of one man and one woman makes divorce unacceptable except in cases of infidelity (Matthew 5:31-32). Likewise, God forbids adultery and premarital sex (Exodus 20:14; Proverbs 6:32; 1 Corinthians 6:18; Hebrews 13:4), homosexual relations (Leviticus 18:22, 20:13; Romans 1:26-27; 1 Corinthians 6:9), and bestiality (Exodus 22:19; Leviticus 18:23; Deuteronomy 27:21). Husbands are admonished to love their wife and not to treat her harshly (Colossians 3:19), while women are reminded to dress modestly in suitable apparel, adorning themselves with good deeds (1 Timothy 2:9).

In conclusion, the tremendous words of Isa's emissary Paul tell us how the wonder of marriage points to still greater wonders.

You husbands, love your wife just as al-Masih loved the community of believers. He gave up his life for her, and having thus washed her clean through his word, he made her pure and holy.

(Ephesians 5:25-36)

How Do the Holy Scriptures Describe the Heavenly Paradise?

Heaven is and will be like this.

A place where Allah will dwell with his people, free from trouble:

> *Look! Allah's dwelling is with mankind! He will live with them, and they will be his people. It is Allah himself who will live with them and be their God. And he will wipe away every tear from their eyes. Death will be no more, and sorrow, crying, and pain will cease. The former things are gone!*
>
> (Revelation 21:3-4)

Where people become immortal and glorious, yet like before:

> Isa al-Masih said, *"At the resurrection people will neither marry nor be given in marriage; they will be like the angels in heaven."*
>
> (Matthew 22:30, NIV)

> *Many of those who sleep in the dusty ground will awake—some to everlasting life, and others to shame and everlasting abhorrence. But the wise will shine like the brightness of the heavenly expanse. And those bringing many to righteousness will be like the stars forever and ever.*
>
> (Daniyal/Daniel 12:2-3, NET)

> *... Isa took Peter, John, and Yaqub up a mountain to pray. And as he was praying, his face changed and his clothes became dazzling white. And suddenly, two men appeared—Musa and Ilyas—talking with Isa. All in glorious splendor, they discussed ....*
>
> (Luke 9:28-31)

A place to worship Allah:

> *Then I looked and heard the voices of many angels. They encircled the throne, the living creatures, and the elders. The angels numbered millions and millions, and they said in a resounding voice, "Worthy is the Lamb who was slaughtered to receive power, riches, wisdom, strength, honor, glory, and praise!" And then I heard every created being, those in heaven and those living on the earth and in the earth and in the sea, every one of them, saying, "To the One who sits on the throne, and to the Lamb, be praise, honor, glory, and authority forever and ever!" Then the four living creatures said, "Amen!," and the elders bowed in worship.*
>
> (Revelation 5:11-14)

New and entirely righteous:

> *... what holy and godly lives you should live, looking forward to the day of God and hurrying it along. On that day, he will set the heavens on fire, and the elements will melt away in the flames. But we are looking forward to the new heavens and new earth he has promised, a world filled with God's righteousness.*
>
> (2 Peter 3:11-13, NLT)

> *Allah said to Prophet Isaiah, "Take note. I will create new heavens and a new earth. The former things will be forgotten and disappear from mind."*
>
> (Isaiah 65:17)

A place of peace and joy:

> *... They will beat their swords into plowshares and their spears into pruning knives. Nations will not take up the sword against nations and no longer train for war. ... You will set out with joy and be led in peace. The mountains and the hills will burst into cheers before you, and all the trees in the fields will clap their hands.*
>
> (Isaiah 2:4; 55:12)

For the humble, not for those who are merely rich or powerful:

> *... the disciples came to Isa and asked, "So, who is the greatest in the kingdom of Heaven?" Isa called to a child and stood him in their midst. Then Isa said, "I tell you the truth, if you do not change and become like this child, you absolutely will not enter into the kingdom of Heaven. Whoever lowers oneself to the position of this child is the greatest in the kingdom of Heaven."*
>
> (Matthew 18:1-4)

> Then Isa said to his disciples, *"Truly I tell you, it is hard for someone who is rich to enter the kingdom of Heaven."*
>
> (Matthew 19:23, NIV)

A place of togetherness:

> *When the time came, Isa and his emissaries sat down together to eat. And Isa said to them, "I've been so eager to eat this Passover with you before I suffer. As for me, I won't eat this meal again until its fulfillment in the kingdom of Allah." Picking up a full cup he thanked Allah for it and said, "Take this and share it among yourselves. As for*

me, I will not drink again from the fruit of the vine until the kingdom of Allah has come."

(Mark 14:22-25)

An inheritance for Allah's spiritual children:

May God, the Father of our Lord Isa al-Masih, be praised! Because he is so merciful, he has given us new life through Isa al-Masih's resurrection after death. His life is our guarantee of an inheritance—entirely secure, untouched by decay, undiminished by time, and kept waiting in heaven for us.

(1 Peter 1:3-4)

Then the sovereignty, authority, and might of the all kingdoms under heaven will be handed over to the holy people of the Most High. His kingdom will be an everlasting one, and he is the one all rulers will worship and obey.

(Daniyal/Daniel 7:27)

A home for each believer:

Isa al-Masih said to his disciples, *"Don't let your hearts be troubled. Believe in God and also in me. My Father's house has many rooms. If that were not true, I wouldn't tell you I'm leaving to prepare a place for you. And since I'm leaving to prepare you a place, I'll return to take you with me, so that where I am you may be too."*

(John 14:1-3)

Isa's emissary Paul wrote, *"The place of our citizenship is heaven, and from there we eagerly wait for a savior, the Lord Isa al-Masih."*

(Philippians 3:20)

A place to live forever:

Isa al-Masih said, *"Everyone who hears and learns from the Father comes to me. ... I tell you the truth, whoever believes has eternal life. I am the bread of life. ... I am the living bread which comes down from heaven. Whoever eats this bread will live forever."*

(John 6:45, 47-48, 51)

Whoever is victorious, I will allow to eat from the tree of life which is in the Paradise of Allah.

(Revelation 2:7)

What Should We Think About Politics and Government?

We are beset by unsolvable problems. Selfishness and death rank at the top, turning human history, especially political history, into mere wanderings. A cynic might describe government like this:

> Flawed people ruling a flawed populace in a flawed place.
> One ego telling another ego how to live.
> Washing a mud floor.

The mother of two brothers, both Isa's disciples, came to him with a request. Her sons probably sent her. She asked that in heaven they be made highest in command, second only to Isa. The other ten disciples became upset. Isa went on to tell them all this:

> *You know that the rulers of the Gentiles lord it over them, and their high officials exercise authority over them. Not so with you. Instead, whoever wants to become great among you must be your servant, and whoever wants to be first must be your slave—just as the Son of Man did not come to be served, but to serve, and to give his life as a ransom for many.*
>
> (Matthew 20:25-28, NIV)

Despite its many weaknesses, human government tends to be the lesser of two evils. Anarchy and chaos are usually worse. During the life of Isa, and for many generations after, Rome ruled a large part of the ancient world. It was brutal to those who defied it, but Rome also brought a sense of order under which many people lived relatively stable lives. Here is part of Allah's command through Isa's emissary Paul to believers:

> *Everyone should submit to governing authorities, for all authority derives from Allah, and those which exist have been appointed by him. ... A ruler is Allah's servant designed for your good. If you do wrong, you should be afraid. For that very reason, as Allah's servant, he bears the sword to execute punishment on those who do wrong.*
>
> (Romans 13:1, 4)

Allah's command through Isa's emissary Peter is similar:

> *For the Lord's sake submit to every human authority. That may be a ruling king or governors sent by him, those who punish wrongdoers but honor people who do right. For when foolish people make baseless accusations against you, doing what's right is the way Allah wants you to silence them. Though you are free, you are Allah's servants. So*

don't use your freedom as a cloak for evil. Honor everyone, love fellow believers, fear Allah, and honor the king.

(1 Peter 2:13-17)

Of course, when rulers require us to do evil, we cannot obey them, and we may have to bear the consequences. An ancient Babylonian king required that all his people worship a gold idol. Three Hebrews politely refused and were thrown into a huge fire. But Allah protected them and they survived (Daniyal/Daniel 3). Likewise, some followers of Isa would not worship the Roman ruler. They were sentenced to death and killed by beheading, fire or wild animals. History tells us that Isa's emissary Peter was crucified for his faith. Emissary Paul, being a Hebrew with Roman citizenship, was probably beheaded. He accepted his pending fate because, as he put it, "our citizenship is in heaven" (Philippians 3:20, NET).

Some religious leaders tried to trick Isa into creating trouble for himself. Should he compromise his beliefs by paying taxes to a pagan Roman government, or should he compromise his life by breaking Roman law? Isa would have none of such sophistry. He answered this way:

"You hypocrites, why are you trying to trap me? Show me the coin used for paying the tax." They brought him a denarius, and he asked them, "Whose image is this? And whose inscription?" "Caesar's," they replied. Then he said to them, "So give back to Caesar what is Caesar's, and to God what is God's."

(Matthew 22:18-21, NIV)

Much could be said about our relationship with government, and each of us should carefully consider our own situation and circumstances. But after that, we should remember the great people of faith who've gone before us. The sufferings they endured, often at the hands of unjust rulers, taught them a great truth:

All those people died strong in faith. They hadn't received Allah's promises, but as if seeing them from afar, they greeted them and admitted that on earth they were but migrants and exiles. People who say such things reveal their desire for a homeland. Now, if they were thinking of a place they had left, they could have simply returned to it. But they longed for something better—heaven itself. Therefore Allah is not ashamed to be known as their God, and for them he's prepared a city.

(Hebrews 11:13-16)

What Is Prayer?

Prayer is a very simple thing: communication with Allah ta'ala. Though often directed heavenward, from man to God, the reverse can also be true. Therefore, prayer is not a mere repetition of words, a position of the body or a means to participate in a religious society. Prayer is the human heart before its maker. It is appropriate any time and ideally, all the time.

Second, though Allah hears the prayers of all who sincerely call upon him (Zabur/Psalm 145:18), to those who know him, he becomes like a loving father, even while retaining his exalted status as God Almighty whom we can comprehend only in part. In fact, fatherhood began not with the birth of human babies, but through the Most High himself (Ephesians 3:14-15). The more we know and follow his ways, the more we understand him to be our spiritual Father, the creator of our souls. Isa al-Masih, therefore, said this about prayer:

> *... when you pray, don't be a hypocrite, like those who love to stand and pray so visibly in prayer halls and on street corners. They simply want others to notice them. ... Instead, enter a secluded room, shut the door, and pray to your unseen Father. Then, your Father who sees what is done in secret will reward you. And do not prattle on like pagans, who imagine their lengthy prayers will attract Allah's attention. Don't imitate them, for your Father knows what you need before you ask him. So, this is how you should pray: "Our Father in heaven ...."*
>
> (Matthew 6:5-9)

Isa also said this about prayer:

> *"And so I tell you, keep asking and you will receive. Keep seeking, and you will find. Keep knocking, and the door will be opened to you. For everyone who asks, receives, and everyone who seeks, finds, and to everyone who knocks, the door will be opened. You who are fathers, if your son asks for a fish, do you instead hand him a snake? Or if he asks for an egg, do you give him a scorpion? So if you, sinful as you are, know how to give good gifts to your children, how much more will your heavenly Father give his Holy Spirit to those who ask him."*
>
> (Luke 11:9-13)

Those are the basics. Sometimes, however, children ask their parents for harmful things. Allah does not promise to give us those. At other times, like foolish children, we wander away from him. We may claim to follow Allah, but we pray only to satisfy our greed and lust. Allah will not answer such prayers (Yaqub/James 4:1-3). Instead, he may draw back or even oppose us, hoping that we change our ways.

> *You adulterous people, don't you know that friendship with the world means enmity against God? ... That is why Scripture says: "God opposes the proud but shows favor to the humble." Submit yourselves, then, to God. Resist Iblis, and he will flee from you. Come near to God and he will come near to you. Wash your hands, you sinners, and purify your hearts, you double-minded. Grieve, mourn and wail. Change your laughter to mourning and your joy to gloom. Humble yourselves before the Lord, and he will lift you up.*
>
> (Yaqub/James 4:4, 6-10)

Finally, there are times when, asking with a pure heart for what is good, Allah says no in lieu of something better. That happened to Paul when he asked for relief from distress (2 Corinthians 12:7-10). Whether with a yes, no, or wait, Allah always responds graciously to the prayers of his children.

What Is Involved in True Religious Life?

Imagine a secret atheist who observes religious requirements to please his parents. They might be satisfied, but not Allah, who is all-knowing. He demands sincerity. A prosperous businessman, though outwardly religious, cleverly cheats his clients. He never gets caught, and people praise him for his religiosity. That might pass in society, but not before Allah. He demands purity. Finally, another man believes in Allah and carefully observes all the laws, rules, and requirements. His religion constrains him to treat people fairly, which he does. But deep down, the man is proud in heart and feels contempt for others. People praise him, but not Allah. He demands humility.

With a bit of effort, people can keep religious requirements. But to truly honor Allah requires far more. Many claim the following five points, principles or pillars are central to true religion: 1) belief, 2) worship, 3) charitable giving, 4) fasting, and 5) pilgrimage. The Holy Scriptures strongly affirm these five points, but to them they add some interesting and provocative twists.

Belief

Religions generally have a creed—an abbreviated set of accepted beliefs. The teachings of the Holy Scriptures center on Isa al-Masih, about whom they say a great deal. One short, poetic form states things this way:

> *"He appeared in a body, was vindicated by the Spirit, was seen by angels, was preached among the nations, was believed on in the world, was taken up in glory."*
>
> (1 Timothy 3:16, NIV)

Another place says this:

> *Remember this: You were bought out of the dead-end life you inherited from your ancestors. But that was not accomplished with mere transitory things such as silver or gold. No, you were rescued by the precious blood of al-Masih, he who was like a perfect, unblemished lamb.*
>
> (1 Peter 1:18-19)

Worship

Prayer five, ten, or even twenty times a day is not enough for Allah. He wants our entire lives. As he told Prophet Ibrahim:

> *"Walk before me faithfully and be blameless."*
>
> (Genesis 17:1)

The Injil tells us to:

> *"Always rejoice. Never stop praying. In every moment be thankful. That is God's will in Isa al-Masih for you."*
>
> (1 Thessalonians 5:16-18)

Our hearts and lives, therefore, should be filled with worship every minute of every day. Allah doesn't need our worship. It is we who need to worship him. Without it, even if we claim to follow the truth, we will inevitably turn to the false gods of wealth, power, fame or pleasure.

Charitable Giving

Isa said some shocking things, and this is one of them:

> *"Whoever comes to me without hating their father, mother, wife, children, brothers, sisters, and even their own life, cannot be my disciple. And whoever does not carry their own cross and follow me, cannot be my disciple. ... unless you give up everything you have, you cannot be my disciple."*
>
> (Luke 14:26, 27, 33)

At the very least Isa means that nothing comes before Allah; everything we possess is subject to his rule. Giving to those in need is a natural result, a mere part of an entire life owned by our Lord and Master.

Fasting

Isa al-Masih called his followers to fast (Matthew 9:14-15). Sadly, many of them today do little of it and could take an example from other religions. But beyond mere periodic fasting from food or drink, Isa demands an entire life of fasting from ego and self. He said this about himself:

> *"For I have come down from heaven not to do my will but to do the will of him who sent me."*
>
> (John 6:38, NIV)

For that reason, he told his disciples something similar:

> *"Kings rule over the nations, and people with authority call themselves benefactors. But you must be different. The greatest among you should consider themselves the youngest, and the leaders, servants. Who is more important, a person at the table, or a servant? The one at the table, right? But I'm here with you as a servant."*
>
> (Luke 22:25-27)

Isa also said,

> *"The Son of Man did not come to be served but to serve, and to give up his life as a ransom for many."*
>
> (Matthew 20:28)

Pilgrimage

The Injil records an incident where, as Isa and his disciples were walking to another town, someone came up to Isa and said:

> *... "I'll follow you wherever you go." But Isa warned, "Foxes have dens, and birds have nests, but the Son of Man has no place to lay his head."*
>
> (Luke 9:57-58)

Isa taught that our entire life on earth is one of pilgrimage. The only true holy place is heaven, the throne room of Allah. Mature believers admit that on earth they are:

> *... but migrants and exiles. People who say such things reveal their desire for a homeland. Now, if they were thinking of a place they had left, they could have simply returned to it. But they longed for something better—heaven itself. Therefore Allah is not ashamed to be known as their God, and for them he's prepared a city ....*
>
> (Hebrews 11:13-16)

What Can We Know About the Unseen World of Spirits?

The Holy Scriptures teach that an unseen world of spirits surrounds us. It is both real and powerful. The magic of Pharaoh's servants was genuine, but the power Allah gave Prophet Musa was greater (Exodus 7:1–8:19). While various people, some with and some without Allah's consent, may actively engage this invisible world, no one's authority can compare to that of Isa al-Masih.

> *When Isa went to Peter's home, he saw Peter's mother-in-law lying ill with fever. Isa touched her hand and the fever left. Then she got up and made him a meal. When evening came, people brought him many individuals who were possessed by demons. He cast out the spirits with a word and healed all who were sick. In this way, what Prophet Isaiah said was fulfilled: "He took away our sicknesses, and carried off our diseases."*
>
> (Matthew 8:14-17; see also Luke 11:14-26)

Isa gave similar power to his twelve emissaries (Matthew 10:1). After he was killed, came back to life, and had gone into heaven, his power was available not only to the twelve apostles (e.g., Acts 3:1-10), but also to other disciples (e.g., Acts 6:8; 8:4-13; 13:4-12; 19:11-20; 1 Corinthians 12:27-31). More damaging than physical ills are the false teachings promoted by demons through people (1 Timothy 4:1). While there are bad spirits, there are also good spirits known as angels. They sometimes assist and even visit Allah's people (Acts 12:1-19; Hebrews 1:13-14; 13:2). This whole topic is a large one and deserves careful study. A few more key concepts will have to suffice here. Specifically, Allah gives his people clear warnings, assistance, instructions, and encouragement.

A warning:

> *Stay alert and attentive. Your enemy Iblis prowls around like a roaring lion looking for prey to devour. Resist him by standing strong in your faith. And remember that your brothers and sisters elsewhere in the world are enduring the same kinds of sufferings. Allah, the source of all kindness, called you through Isa al-Masih to experience his eternal glory. So after you have suffered a little while, Allah himself will restore, support, strengthen, and establish you.*
>
> (1 Peter 5:8-10)

Divine assistance:

Finally, be mighty in the Lord through his great power. Gird yourselves with all the battle gear from Allah so you can stand strong against Iblis' schemes. For the combat we face is not against mere flesh-and-blood humans, but against celestial forces—rulers, authorities, cosmic leaders of this dark place, and malicious spiritual beings in the heavens. Therefore, to stand firm in evil times, equip yourself with all Allah's battle gear. Then, having been fully prepared, you will be able to stand firm. So stand firm! Know the truth, buckled on like a soldier's belt. Live a righteous life, for it will guard you like a breastplate. March forth with the good news of peace, as on well-shod feet. Always carry faith as your shield, for it will extinguish all the evil one's flaming arrows. Don your salvation like a helmet. In your hand carry the word of Allah, the sword granted you by his Spirit. Pray in every situation, always appealing through his Spirit. And devote yourselves diligently to prayer as you petition for all Allah's people.

(Ephesians 6:10-18)

Instructions and encouragement:

Dear ones, don't believe every spirit-inspired message. Instead, test every spirit to determine if it is from Allah. For many false prophets have gone out into the world. Here's how you can know the Spirit of Allah. Whenever a spirit professes that Isa Al-Masih has come as a man, that is the Spirit come from Allah. But any spirit which does not profess Isa is not from Allah. That is an anti-Masih spirit. You've heard that such a thing is coming, and in fact it's already in the world. You, dear children, are from Allah. And you've overcome the false prophets because greater is the One in you than the one in the world. The others belong to this world, so they speak of worldly things, and the world heeds them. We are from Allah. Anyone who knows him listens to us. Anyone not from Allah does not listen to us. So this is how we distinguish the Spirit which speaks truth from a spirit which deceives.

(1 John 4:1-6)

Are the Holy Scriptures Trustworthy? What About the Words of Isa al-Masih in Them?

No ancient religion possesses its original scriptures, first written on rock, clay, wood, bone, paper, animal skin, or the like. The originals were copied and later lost, buried, or destroyed. The same is true of most ancient texts and even of many more modern books and writings. Furthermore, some scriptures were written not by the prophets themselves, but by those who claimed to have heard them. From this we see that no matter the religion, a measure of faith is required in the trustworthiness of its writings. Claims are made about holy texts, but none of us possess the original, imperishable, writings descended directly from heaven. We are left with belief that what we possess are holy words revealed ages ago.

Put another way, it is impossible to scientifically prove that any religious scriptures available today came to us directly from Allah via his angels or prophets. Claiming divine descent, however vehemently, does not make it so. Sincere conviction, history, logic, traditions, or threats may convince people. They might even convince the vast majority of people, especially in tight-knit societies. But such methods can at best turn skepticism into faith, not into fact.

When it comes to the Holy Injil, literally thousands of ancient, hand-written copies or portions still exist today. The oldest are over 1,800 years old, coming to within a few decades of the original authors' lives. Many are 1,600 to 1,700 years old, predating later religions and their own revelations. All these many manuscripts testify to people's great enthusiasm for the good news about Isa. People were so excited they copied the Injil whenever they could. Meaningful differences between the manuscripts are minor, usually in spelling and word order. The science of textual studies compares the differences, evaluates them, and brings the words of the Injil to almost complete certainty. The few places where questions might remain make no difference to the truth about Isa. The many copies show that nothing of substance is missing, nothing material has been added, and nothing significant was changed. In the relatively few places that remain, it's a matter of deciding which of two or three often very similar forms is the original. Yes, faith is required, but at least the issues—minor though they may be—are transparent for the entire world to see.

It is a dangerous diversion to state that the Injil has been corrupted while ignoring its message based on the entirety of the manuscript tradition. Faith is still required of any religion, even those which claim their ancient texts have no variations. Encouraging such faith in the Holy Scriptures, Isa spoke about the trustworthiness of the Tawrat, the Prophets, and the Zabur, as well as the Injil:

> *"I tell you the truth, until heaven and earth disappear, not even the smallest detail of Allah's law will disappear until its purpose is achieved. ... Heaven and earth will disappear, but my words will never disappear."*
>
> (Matthew 5:18; Matthew 24:35)

Some unbelievers claim that Isa al-Masih was a liar. Some, that he was a lunatic. Let us not join their ranks with the dishonoring legend that his words have been lost. It is a fearful thing to teach that the Injil is corrupted, that Allah has not preserved the truth he proclaimed through his holy prophet. For those tempted to make such unsupported claims, it is worth remembering Isa's words:

> *"Listen to me, on the Day of Judgment people will give an account for every useless thing they have said."*
>
> (Matthew 12:36)

The real questions are not about the trustworthiness of the Holy Scriptures, but about the meaning of their content. In particular, who was Isa al-Masih, what did he say and do, and how should that affect my life and beliefs? As some shrewd military men of his day noted, "No one has ever spoken like this!" (John 7:46). Mere humans could not have invented the life and teaching of Isa as we read it in the Holy Injil.

When it comes to faith—confidence in the truth about Isa al-Masih—Isa himself tells us clearly:

> *"Anyone who wants to do what Allah desires will know whether my teaching is from him or is merely my own."*
>
> (John 7:17)

"Anyone" includes you and me.

What about translations of holy books in general? Don't they corrupt the original? Not necessarily. Allah made language, and he can help people translate his Holy Scriptures. Just before returning to heaven:

> *Isa went over to his disciples and spoke to them, saying, "I have been given all authority in heaven and on earth. Therefore, go and make disciples of all peoples, ritually washing them in the name of the Father and the Son and Allah's Holy Spirit. Teach them to obey all the commands I have given you. And be sure of this: I am with you always, to the end of the world."*
>
> (Matthew 28:18-20)

Isa likely said that in Aramaic. His disciples wrote his words in Greek. Since then they have been translated into thousands of languages, more than any other book. Allah can help translators convey his holy message, for in Isa, the greatest of all translations, we see the Almighty himself.

> *Philip said to Isa, "Lord, show us the Father. Then we'll be satisfied." Isa replied, "Philip, how could I have been with you all this time and you not know me? Anyone who has seen me has seen the Father. So why do you ask me to show him to you? Don't you believe that I am in the Father and the Father is in me? The things I tell you are not my own. The Father, living in me, does his work. Believe me when I say I am in the Father and the Father is in me. Or believe simply because of the things I've done. I tell you the truth, anyone who believes in me will do the same things I have done and even greater still, because I am leaving to be with the Father. If you ask anything in my name, I will do it so that the Father might be glorified through the Son. Whatever you ask me in my name, I will do it!"*
>
> (John 14:8-14)

What Is the True Name of the Most High?

Before we answer that, it would help to talk about language. There are about 7,000 languages spoken today. Since God is omniscient, he knows them all. Before the tower of Babel, thousands of years before Isa walked on earth, people spoke only one language (Genesis 11:1-9). No one knows what language that was. It might have died out then and there. Even if a descendant language exists, no speaker of it would understand its ancient ancestor. Languages change every generation. That makes literature several hundred years old difficult to read. Literature several thousand years old is impossible to understand today without special information.

What language does the Most High speak? Every language. What language did he speak before humans existed? No one knows. Maybe he spoke a near infinite number of languages. Maybe he didn't even speak like we understand the term. After all, the Almighty doesn't have a tongue, lips, teeth, and vocal cords like we do.

We can talk about and even debate this question. But more important than any pronunciation of any word is the actual meaning of the term God. There is only one Supreme Being. He is the creator of the world—all knowing and all powerful.

Even though people may not know Arabic or English or Chinese, Allah understands their language. He said the following about himself:

> *God does not view things the way men do. People look on the outward appearance, but the LORD looks at the heart.*
>
> (1 Samuel 16:7, NET)

That goes for language, too. The Most High God is not concerned with teaching people how to pronounce foreign words, but how to live, act, think, and believe. Words are simple enough to mimic. Allah is concerned with deeper things, not the movements of our tongue and lips but the movements of our heart.

Allah[a] refers to the one and only God in Arabic. It's a beautiful name. Aramaic and Hebrew have similar words. But God revealed a different divine name to Prophet Musa, *Yahweh* (Exodus 3:14). Though distinct in sound, it

a The etymology of *Allah* in Arabic is disputed. A very widespread theory is that *Allah* arose by fusing the Arabic article *al* with the generic word for God/god, *ilah*. On the other hand, many western scholars believe that the Syriac word for God, *Alaha* was taken into Arabic from Syriac neighbors and became *Allah*. *Alaha* itself was a later form of the Aramaic word for God/god used in the Holy Scriptures (Daniyal/ Daniel 2:18, Mark 15:34) and closely related to the Hebrew words for God/god, i.e., *el*, *eloah*, and *Elohim*. In any case *Allah* is a word that both Arabic-speaking Muslims and Christians have used for more than a thousand years to refer to the one true God despite differences in understanding who he is.

also has a beautiful meaning: "the One who is." Up until recently, a small group of people living in Southeast Asia had no alphabet. None of them wrote or read their own language. But they were not without a beautiful name for God: *Mugbabaya*—"the Ruler over all." It's the meaning of a word that counts. Whatever the language and however we might pronounce the Creator's name, unless the word springs from a pure heart, what rolls off the lips means nothing to him. As the Scriptures say,

> *The LORD is near to all who call on him,*
> *to all who call on him in truth.*
>
> (Zabur/Psalm 145:18, NIV)

What About Warfare?

In a sense, war began in the Garden of Eden. There, Adam and Hawwa listened to the lies of Shaitan and defied Allah's clear commands (Genesis 3). Later, Hawwa's first son murdered his younger brother, and humanity has been fighting ever since. Many Old Testament believers in Allah, both kings and prophets, took part in war. At best, war is a necessity due to the presence of evil. As the Scriptures say,

> *For everything there is a season, a time for every activity under heaven. ... A time to love and a time to hate. A time for war and a time for peace.*
>
> (Ecclesiastes 3:1, 8, NLT)

When evil people hurt the innocent, they should be stopped. Sometimes Allah himself does so, as he did via the ancient flood (Genesis 6–8) and with the cities of Sodom and Gomorrah (Genesis 18–19). At other times, he expects people to step in. When and how that should happen is not always easy to say.

In ancient times, the kingdom of Israel was to be a theocracy—a people ruled by Allah himself. He wanted them to purge the great evil out of the land they were to inhabit, and that initially meant war. But war was not supposed to be a continual practice. Once the cleansing of the land was completed, fighting was to diminish or end. Later, Israel turned from Allah and wanted a mere human king to rule them. Those kings sometimes fought as Allah had commanded, but more often than not they were simply motivated by foolish thinking.

When Isa came, he used a whip to cleanse the temple in al-Quds. But beyond that, he rejected aggressive warfare and violence. The following occurred just before he was killed.

> *Men approached, grabbed Isa and arrested him. Then one of the men with Isa reached for his sword and drew it out. He struck the servant of the high priest, cutting off an ear. But Isa said to him, "Put your sword back into its place. For those who take up the sword will die by the sword. Don't you realize I can call on my Father and in an instant he'll send me thousands of angels! But if I do, how will the Scriptures be fulfilled which say things must happen as they are?"*
>
> (Matthew 26:50-54)

A few hours later, when standing before the Roman judge who finally condemned him to death, Isa said:

> *"My kingdom is not in this world. If it were, my followers would wage jihad so I wouldn't be turned over to the Jews. No, my kingdom is not here."*
>
> (John 18:36)

Prophet Yahya did not condemn soldiers for their work (Luke 3:14), and neither did Isa (Matthew 8:5-13). Isa's great emissary Paul instructed the believers to obey their rulers, part of a government's responsibility being to "bear the sword" (Romans 13:1-7). On the other hand, there is no teaching in the Injil about pursuing violence to advance the kingdom of Allah. The sword may bring subjection but not sincerity.

Nevertheless, some followers of Isa have misapplied his teachings and wrongly gone out to war. Throughout history, people of all faiths have believed that God called them to advance his purposes by violence. We should not be surprised. All political systems have also been responsible for war, death, and destruction. And some of the world's most violent offenders have been atheists. It is the morally corrupt state of humanity, not "religion," and certainly not Isa, which is responsible for murder and mayhem. Isa allows for none of it, and his followers who have done otherwise, including many during the time of the Crusades, were confused, misled, and wrong.

Why Do We Need a Sacrifice? Can't Allah Just Forgive?

Although we say "Allah is almighty and can do anything," there are some things the Most High cannot do.

Imagine a just policeman who is being bribed. Suppose he says, "Accepting your money would be against the law. I cannot do it." By that he does not mean he is physically unable to accept the money. He would only need to stick out his hand.

Though obviously much greater, Allah ta'ala is like a good policeman. He cannot sin because he will not sin. If Allah did wrong, he would cease being good. Likewise, if the Most High were to let sin go unpunished, he would violate his integrity. Therefore, because Allah is righteous, he always requires justice.

Suppose a brutal, murderous dictator is arrested and tried. And suppose the judge, after hearing all the arguments, rules like this: "The evidence proves that this man has done many terrible things. He has murdered our fellow citizens and even some of our own relatives. But I'm in a good mood today, so I'm going to set him free. He may return to his position. Hopefully he will not murder again. But if he does, oh well. C'est la vie. That's life."

If we lived in such a place, we would feel insulted, angry, and treated unjustly. We would consider the judge to be as evil as the dictator. Allah feels about our sins like we would about the dictator's. The Creator cannot simply ignore wrong or forgive what we've done.

On the other hand, suppose that we ourselves stand before a righteous judge. And suppose he says to us: "In my courtroom, not only are murderers found guilty, those who want to murder are also guilty. Not only are thieves condemned, so are those who covet the possessions of others. Not only are convicted liars sentenced, so are all those who have lied about anything. Not only are ...." In such a courtroom, none of us would be set free.

So it is with Allah. Even though he is almighty, his holiness requires that he cannot simply forgive us, no matter how small our sins might seem. A pardon for sin might appear to be the nice thing to do, but to the Most High it is plainly wrong, letting evil go unpunished. Allah can forgive us only because the price for our wrong has been paid. How? Because justice has been served by the sacrifice of Isa al-Masih, the unblemished lamb of Allah, who poured out his blood to pay for all our sins (John 1:29, 1 Peter 1:18-19). For as we saw in the discussion about Isa's death:

> *... he was pierced for our transgressions, he was crushed for our iniquities; the punishment that brought us peace was on him, and by his wounds we are healed. We all, like sheep, have gone astray, each of us has turned to our own way; and the LORD has laid on him the iniquity of us all.*
>
> (Isaiah 53:5, 6, NIV)

Why Should I Follow a Religious Faith?

Everyone believes in something. Atheists believe there is no God, even one that might be hiding in the dark corners of the vast cosmos. Other people don't care about the question, believing it doesn't matter one way or another. So we might say that everyone has a religious faith. But most people believe in God. Why? Because, as the Holy Scriptures say,

> *From the moment the world was made, the unseen essence of Allah—his eternal power and divinity—have been obvious when observing the creation. As a result, people have no excuse.*
>
> (Romans 1:20)

Belief in God makes sense, in large part because of the evidence all around us. Take, for example, the beauty of a flower or the incredible complexity of life. But what kind of faith should we follow? After all, there are many religions. The answer to that question is not simple, and it deserves our utmost attention.

People often believe for the wrong reasons, such as:

To fit in with society. But strong people want truth more than they merely want to fit in.
Just in case. But Allah wants sincere believers, not people looking for an insurance policy.
Pressure. But faith is too important to simply believe what others tell us.
To feel better about themselves. That may be a result of faith, but it's too small to be the foundation.
Because their parents do. But what if our parents also believed for the same reason?
To find a good spouse. Though important, marriage is small compared to eternity.

If we believe for one of those reasons—even if what we believe is right—we're people of faith in name only, not in heart. There's a word for that: hypocrisy. It comes from the ancient Greek language and means to act in a play. In real life, it's not enough to be a good actor. God Most High isn't fooled. We need to be sincere. To do that, we must scrutinize what we've heard and search for what is right. As the Scriptures say,

> *"For I know the plans I have for you," declares the LORD, "plans to prosper you and not to harm you, plans to give you hope and a future. Then you will call on me and come and pray to me, and I will listen*

to you. You will seek me and find me when you seek me with all your heart."

(Jeremiah 29:11-13, NIV)

The God who made the world and everything in it is the Lord of heaven and earth and does not live in temples built by human hands. And he is not served by human hands, as if he needed anything. Rather, he himself gives everyone life and breath and everything else. From one man he made all the nations, that they should inhabit the whole earth; and he marked out their appointed times in history and the boundaries of their lands. God did this so that they would seek him and perhaps reach out for him and find him, though he is not far from any one of us. "For in him we live and move and have our being."

(Acts 17:24-28, NIV)

Sincere seekers will examine both the words and the life of the world's religious leaders. Among them, Isa is universally recognized as one of the greatest. When you consider him, you'll see that he doesn't give us the freedom to hold wildly different opinions about him. He forces us to consider him either a liar (but that's unlikely, given that he died for his beliefs), a madman (that's also unlikely, given that he lived such a consistently good life), or he is who he claimed to be—our Lord, the Son of the Most High, the Messiah, and the savior of all who go to him.

Choosing a faith can cost us a great deal, even our earthly life. Many of Isa's disciples have been persecuted and a considerable number killed because of their faith. But compared to eternity, this life—precious though it may be—is small.

Why Are There Four Gospels?

Gospel is an old English word meaning "good news." It's a translation of a Greek word, *euanggelion*, from which later came the Arabic word *Injil*. Matthew, Mark, Luke, and John are the four Gospel accounts of the life of Isa al-Masih. They are collected together at the beginning of the Injil, itself the final volume of the Holy Scriptures.

Isa's emissaries Matthew and John witnessed his ministry from its inception through his death and resurrection. Mark, a younger man present at least during the later events of Isa's life, was taught by Isa's emissary and eyewitness Peter. *The Good News According to Luke*, written under the inspiration of Allah's Holy Spirit, is a report by a meticulous historian who claimed to have "carefully investigated everything from the beginning" (Luke 1:3). Luke no doubt learned from many of the other eyewitnesses, among them Maryam, the mother of Isa.

But why, we might ask, are four accounts necessary? Furthermore, given differences among them, doesn't their very multiplicity imply that they negate one another?

The following is an important truth given to us by Prophet Musa. It was quoted or referred to numerous times throughout the Holy Scriptures, and even by Isa himself (Matthew 18:16).

> *A claim must be confirmed by the testimony of two or three witnesses.*
> (Deuteronomy 19:15)

The four different accounts of the good news first of all show us how Allah keeps his own word. When it comes to his most important revelation—that about Isa al-Masih—Allah didn't give us one account from an isolated individual. Instead, the Most High teaches us about the vast richness of Isa's life through multiple prophet-witnesses. Furthermore, Allah works through well-documented and verifiable history, not merely through private revelations to a single person. The prophetic witnesses of the Gospels uphold the truth that Allah himself is speaking. Each account of the good news confirms and supports the others. As we learned in the discussion about the death of Isa, additional people who lived during his life and soon thereafter also wrote about him. Statements by individuals born centuries later cannot negate established testimony concerning what these earlier people saw, learned, and passed on. For those reasons, the four Gospels should be seen as a strong confirmation from Allah. Given the instructions above from the law of Musa, they make the "claim" about Isa thoroughly "confirmed."

Second, the four accounts of the good news in no way contradict each other. They simply tell from different perspectives the facts about the world's most incredible person. In a courtroom, if the testimonies of two or more people are identical, a good judge will accuse the speakers of collusion and throw them all out. A strong case is established only when two or more clearly independent witnesses swear to the truth of their distinct, non-contradictory, but parallel statements. Remember the blind men describing an elephant? "A rope!" said one feeling the tail. "A tree trunk!" said another of the leg. "Spears!" said yet another about the tusks. The Gospels go beyond that, for they describe numerous events in Isa's life, and each from a different vantage point. Followers of Isa do not shrink from four Gospel accounts; they rejoice in them. Through the combined witness of the four we see Isa more clearly.

Maps

Roman
Empire
Black Sea
Caspian
Sea
Rome
Carthage
Antioch
Mediterranean Sea
Judea
al-Quds
Alexandria
Red
Sea
The Roman Empire During
the Life of Isa

Land Cover and Vegetation

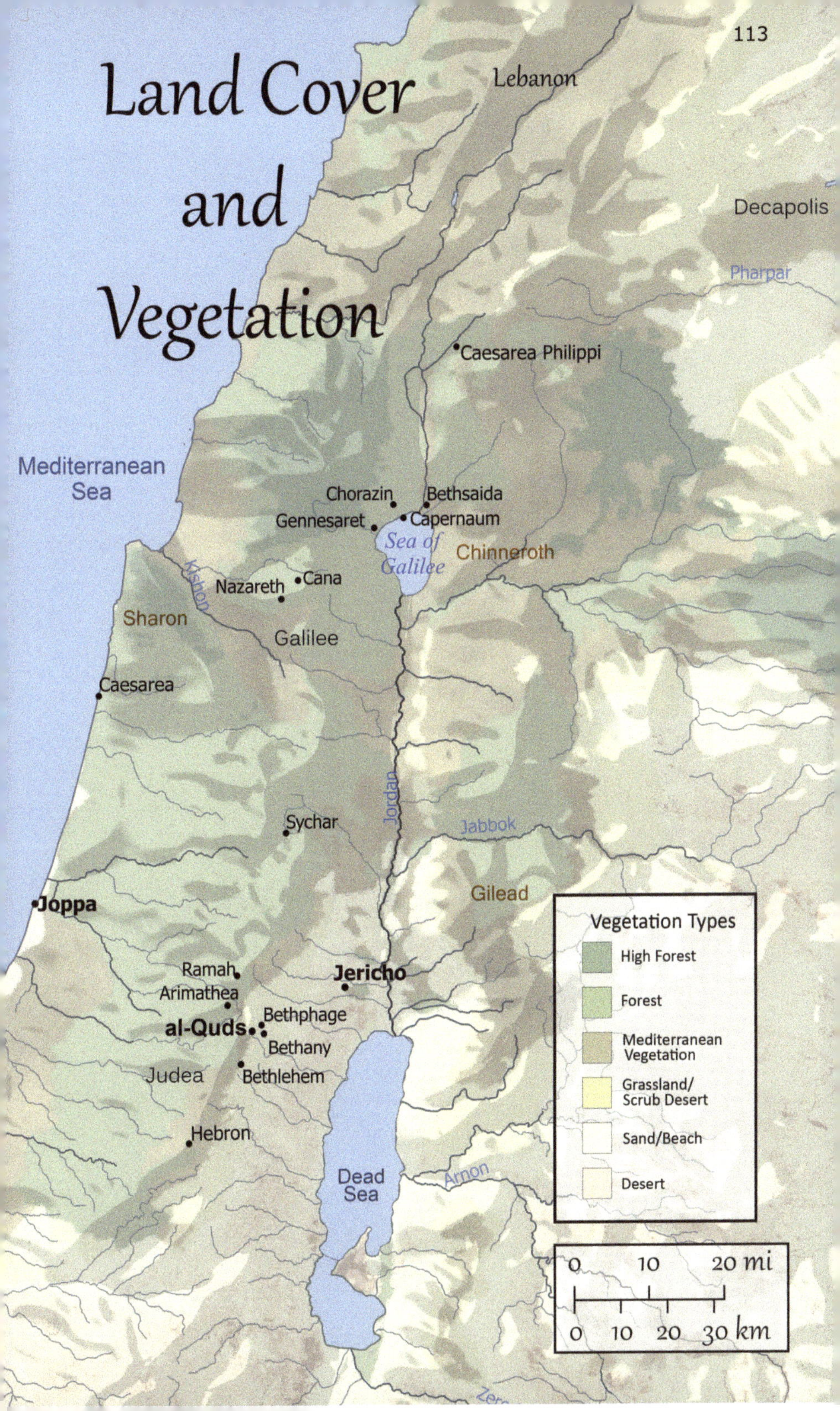

Maryam and Yusuf's Journey to Bethlehem
Lebanon
Sidon
Zarephath
Tyre
Caesarea Philippi
Mediterranean Sea
Chorazin
Bethsaida
Gennesaret
Capernaum
Sea of Galilee
Chinneroth
Kishon
Nazareth
Cana
Sharon
Galilee
Maryam and Yusuf traveled from Nazareth to Bethlehem in order to be registered for the census (Luke 2:1-4).
Caesarea
Jordan
Samaria
Sychar
Jabbok
Joppa
Isa was born in a stable in Bethlehem (Luke 2:5-6).
Gilead
Ramah
Jericho
Arimathea
Bethphage
al-Quds
Bethany
Judea
Bethlehem
Dead Sea
Hebron
Besor
0 10 20 mi
0 10 20 30 km

Isa Amazes the Teachers in the Temple

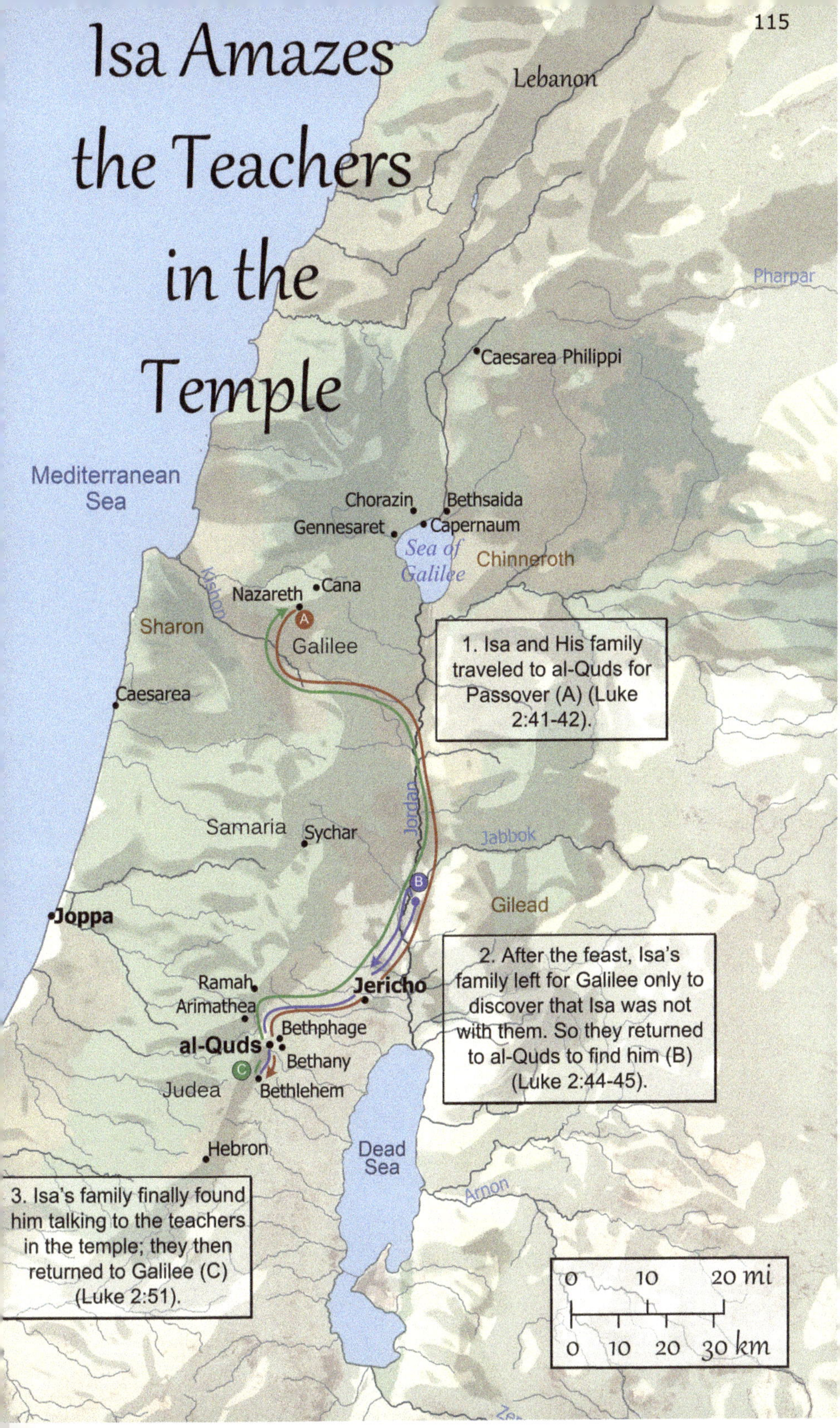

Isa's Ministry Begins: His First Trip to Judea

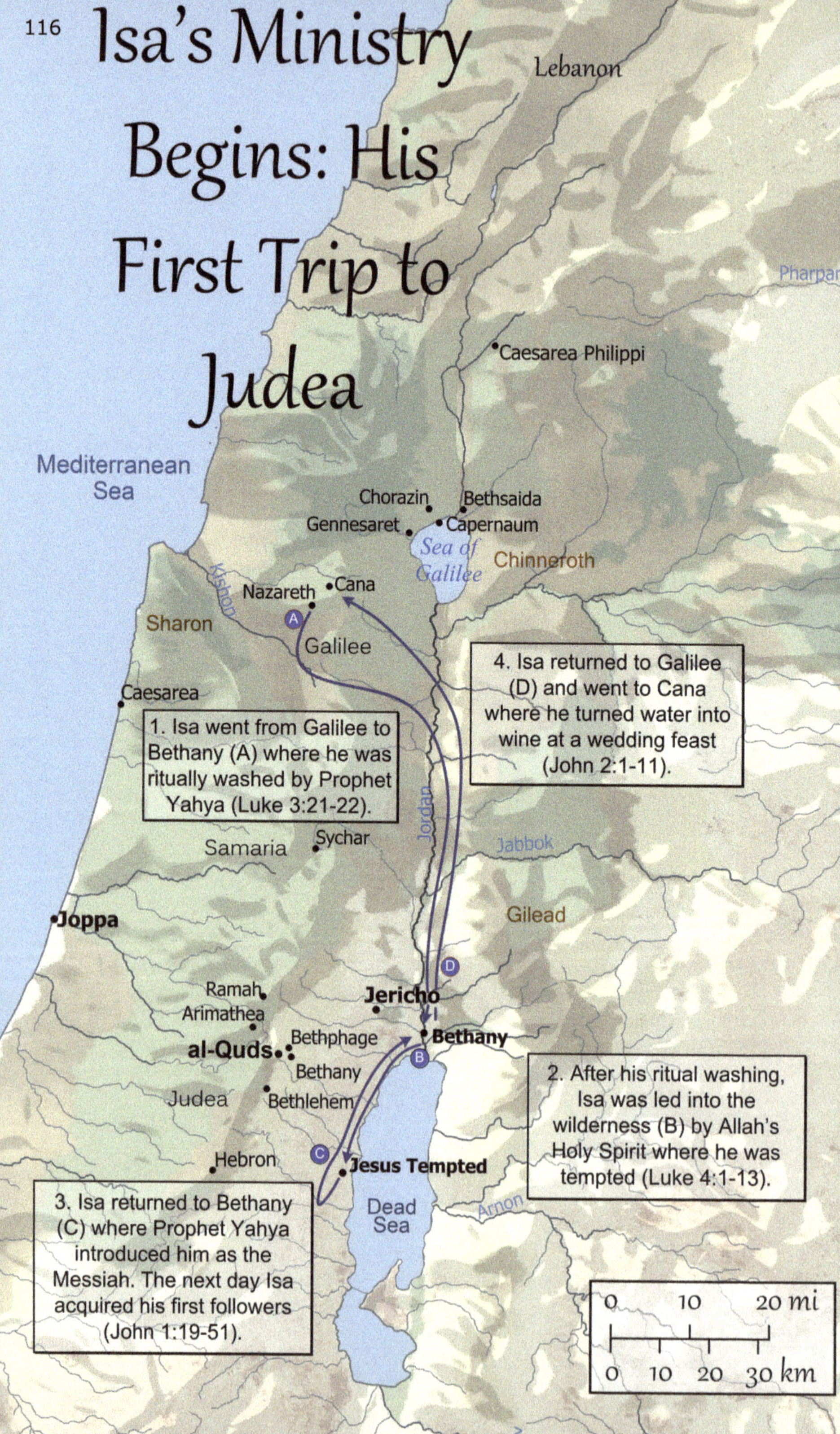

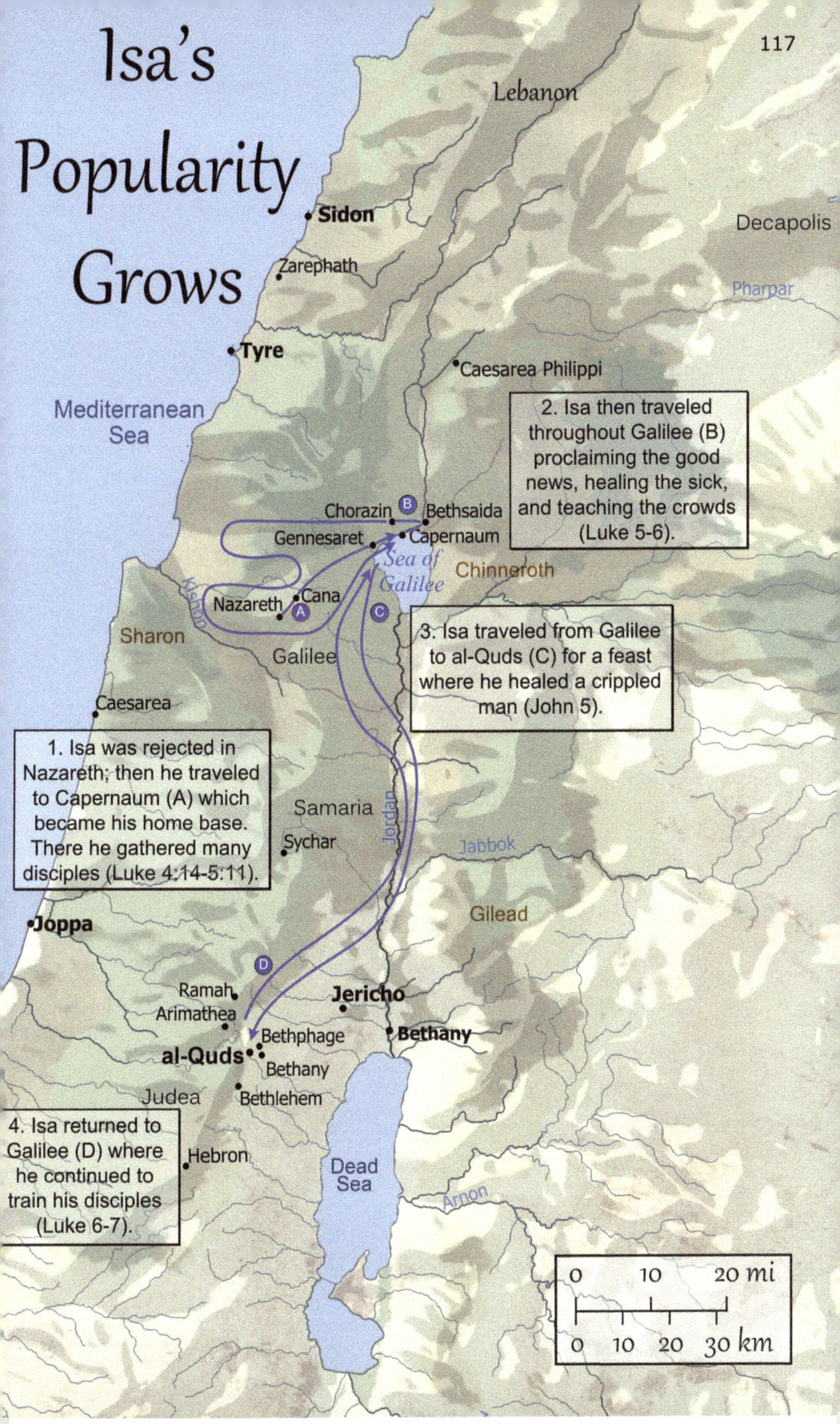
Isa's Popularity Grows
Lebanon
Sidon
Zarephath
Decapolis
Pharpar
Tyre
Caesarea Philippi
Mediterranean Sea
2. Isa then traveled throughout Galilee (B) proclaiming the good news, healing the sick, and teaching the crowds (Luke 5-6).
Chorazin
B
Bethsaida
Gennesaret
Capernaum
Sea of Galilee
Chinneroth
Kishon
Nazareth
Cana
A
C
Sharon
Galilee
3. Isa traveled from Galilee to al-Quds (C) for a feast where he healed a crippled man (John 5).
Caesarea
1. Isa was rejected in Nazareth; then he traveled to Capernaum (A) which became his home base. There he gathered many disciples (Luke 4:14-5:11).
Samaria
Sychar
Jordan
Jabbok
Gilead
Joppa
D
Ramah
Arimathea
Jericho
Bethphage
Bethany
al-Quds
Bethany
Judea
Bethlehem
4. Isa returned to Galilee (D) where he continued to train his disciples (Luke 6-7).
Hebron
Dead Sea
Arnon
0 10 20 mi
0 10 20 30 km

Isa's Final Journey to al-Quds

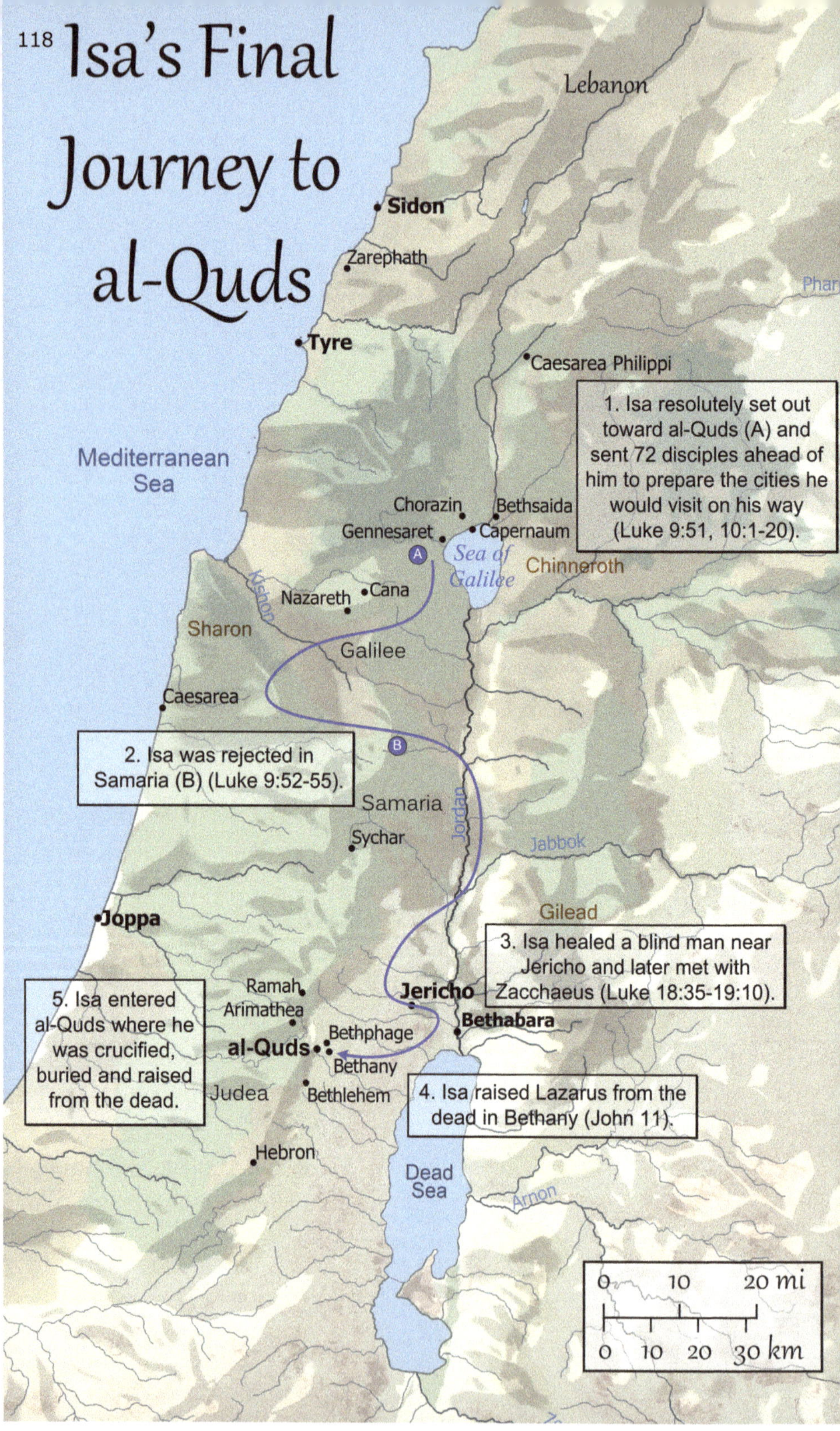

Ancient Manuscript of Luke

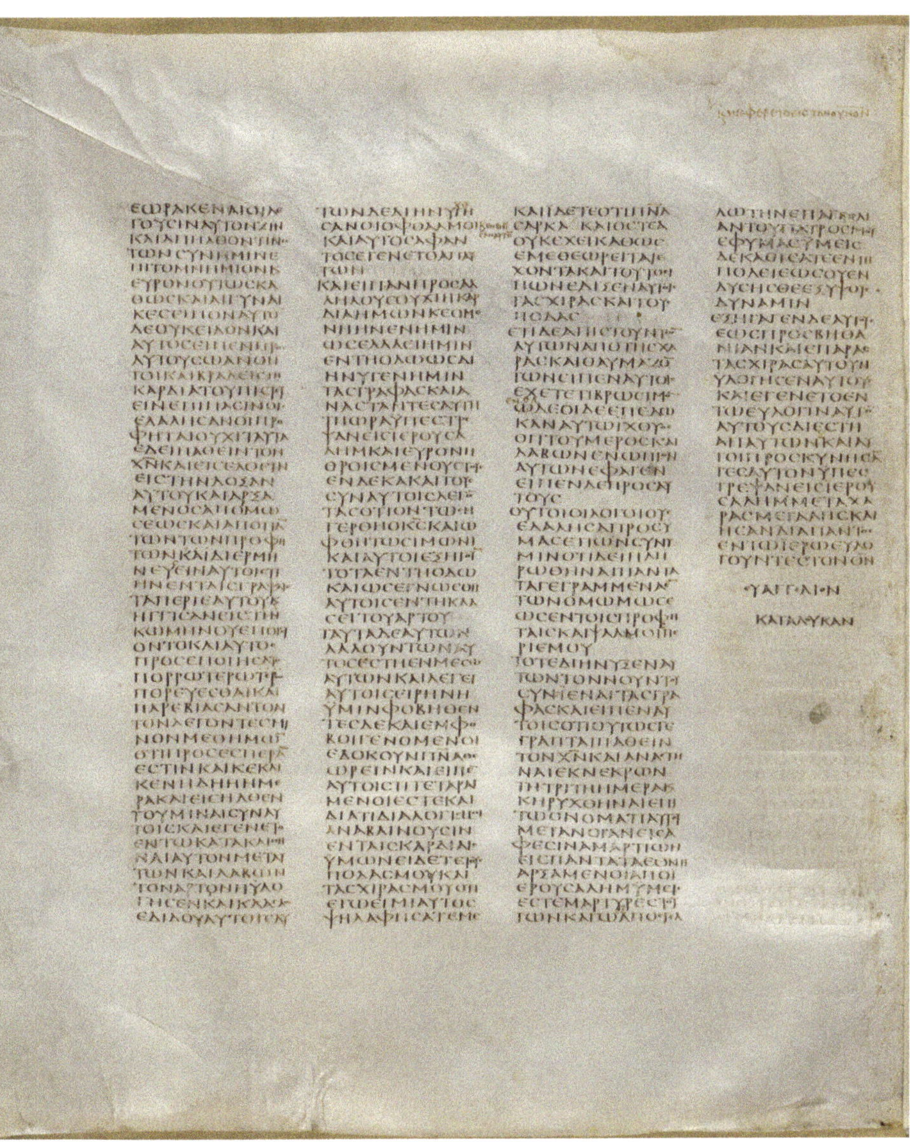

Luke 24:23-53 from Codex Sinaiticus (4th century AD)

www.ingramcontent.com/pod-product-compliance
Ingram Content Group UK Ltd.
Pitfield, Milton Keynes, MK11 3LW, UK
UKHW062257290726
14090UKWH00017B/741